My Tapestry Journey, Certainly Not an Accident!

Marilyn L. Thompson

ISBN 978-1-0980-5075-7 (paperback)
ISBN 978-1-0980-5076-4 (digital)

Christian Faith Publishing, Inc.
832 Park Avenue
Meadville, PA 16335
www.christianfaithpublishing.com

Printed in the United States of America

TAPESTRY is a dramatic operatic musical based on the life of Martin Luther, the sixteenth century Protestant reformer. Over a period of years, I have devoted many hours to writing, orchestrating, and refining this work. Though historically accurate, the fresh uniqueness brought to this theatrical production is really through the dramatization of rarely told joys and sorrows of the reformers. God was indeed working His plan through their intimate relationships during a very tumultuous time in world history.

I never dreamed that a musical endeavor that began primarily as a learning project in orchestration would transform itself into a "magnum opus" and become a constant companion for ten years.

As I began to research Martin Luther, I realized how very little I knew of his relentless search to know a personal and loving God—despite my having grown up in the Protestant church. My enthusiasm and fascination grew by leaps and bounds as I began to express, through music and drama, the story behind the monk who turned the world upside down and ushered in the Protestant Reformation. A trip to Germany and a walk down the streets of Wittenberg provided the visual inspiration that a dramatic musical stage production could be brought to realization.

I am asked sometimes why I have spent so much of my life refining and reworking the musical drama that I have chosen to name **TAPESTRY**. Surely the Protestant Reformation, like much of history, may have faded to irrelevance for a large majority in this modern and progressive society of the twenty-first century!

It is my belief, however, that there are others, albeit perhaps a smaller group, who remain at least curious about the reluctant monk who dared to question Holy Rome and eventually ignite all Europe with the battle cry "By faith alone!" Admittedly, a large majority of today's modern evangelical Christian population may not have thought too much about their historical church roots since they, like myself, did not experience worship in the reformed church tradition.

I owe thanks and appreciation to so many for their contributions and encouragement, but especially to the late Dr. Ovid Young for sharing his wonderful gifts of composition and orchestration through the years and not growing weary of "just one more Luther piece!" Also, a debt of gratitude is owed to world-renowned singer Robert McFarland for his genius in bringing Luther to life with his rich baritone voice in my "make-shift studio." His support and belief that this endeavor was worth carving out the time from his busy schedule of opera performances was invaluable.

Finally, I must say that this has been quite a miraculous, lifelong saga of many twists and turns, not the least of which were two unlikely and totally unrelated chairs playing a pivotal role!

Musical Highlights: https://www.mtmusicministries.com/ Tapestry Excerpts-3-31-2020.mov

For anyone who might consider producing **TAPESTRY**, or desire further information, please contact Marilyn@mtmusicministries.com

Premiere performances were on August 5 and 7, 2016, at the First State Bank Center for the Performing Arts in Gainesville, Texas

"My continuing hope is **TAPESTRY** *will be worthy of future stage performance groups that perhaps may already have the resources for additional staging effects and projected scenery. To visually bring the audience into the actual historical settings will further enhance this unusual story, while adding an exciting new dimension for our modern audiences."*

THIS CHRONICLE OF MEMORIES is lovingly dedicated to my dear husband Bill, who has patiently endured—and perhaps sometimes not so patiently as he would have desired—the sometimes chaotic and unexpected surprises that are just the "status quo" for those of us who appear to most often operate primarily with our right brains. It is also dedicated to our three wonderful children and their young families who are special and unique in their own delightful ways. They are enriching both our lives and the lives of many others while their personal "tapestries" are being woven by God as they travel their own journeys. I also must include a special dedication to my sister Julie Edelberg, whose excellent skill and expertise in proofing enabled my thoughts to be expressed with greater clarity and definition.

PREFACE

ALTHOUGH I CANNOT REMEMBER a time in my childhood and youth that I did not thoroughly enjoy and delight in music, I truly held no obvious promise of professional success in the eyes of many—and "only prodigies need apply!" But God, in His Providence, brought people into my life that, unlike many, saw a spark of creativity somewhere! They were so embracing and gracious in sharing their gifts and imparting their knowledge. They totally changed the path that I would follow!

Who would ever imagine that an old wood saw could be a musical instrument? My first fascination with music began as a five-year-old staring wide eyed while watching a fun-loving African American friend of my parents effortlessly bending the blade of our Dad's wood saw while bowing across the top edge using a violin bow. He was playing a beautiful rendition of the beloved hymn "In the Garden" at our home in Lakewood, California. Jimmy Clark and his wife Lavonia were totally unaware of the surprise baby shower for our mother in progress when they rang the doorbell, but joined right in and became the life of the party with Jimmy providing his unique entertainment! Their yearly Christmas cards were always addressed to "Lakewood's Jimmy Stewart," as there indeed *was* an uncanny resemblance of Dad to the iconic actor!

It seems necessary for me to provide a recounting of this amazing microcosm of my life to further illustrate how Providence was beginning to order my steps so long ago toward the totally unexpected direction that I would follow. What began as a brief narrative has unavoidably become much longer over weeks of writing, since to forget or neglect anyone that God placed in my path would not relate the entire picture of what further along became dubbed "My Tapestry Journey." Regretfully, some of these individuals have already passed from this earthly life. In my mind, however, these memories are still worth sharing if they can bring encouragement to even one person—that God does indeed see the "big picture" even when we do not!

Musicians are often stereotyped as "marching to the beat of a different drummer!" In my case, being fully aware that my musical quest has taken me "off the beaten path" more often than not, I must raise my hand and shout, *"Yes!"*

"ꟿARM UP YOUR FINGERS —since I guess you are it—the new church pianist!" exclaimed Paul, our rather charismatic pastor's son, conjuring up his booming actor's voice to make his point. Paul Shackleton was the very adept choir director at our small church. He also did double duty as a member of the "Birdcage Theater" melodrama players at Knott's Berry Farm in nearby Buena Park, where the many visitors to this famous western theme park were entertained several evenings a week.

The music at Santa Ana First Church of God was of very high quality for a small church, despite the fact that its location was in a not-too-desirable part of town in Orange County, California. The talented pianist, Paul's sister Faythe, was now about to move away to the state of Washington with her new husband, leaving a real void in the music department. I was seventeen at the time I was "drafted," despite being heard at the piano only once when new to the youth group a few months prior. I played a simple chorded accompaniment in that dependable "key of F" for my sisters and me to sing together the old hymn, "I Have Found a Hiding Place." Honestly, my only real skill was that of being able to read music easily.

As I began my tenure as church pianist, Paul, at my insistence, patiently made sure that I had a list of all hymns at least two weeks ahead of every service. My first choir accompaniment consisted of "Spirit of God, Descend upon My Heart" played exactly as written in the hymnal. While beautiful and meaningful, this rendition was rather a simplistic anthem and definitely not on the level of what this fine musician was used to directing. However, he had no alternative but to start from "square one!" I was not at all confident, and the art of improvisation was pretty much unknown to me. My only instruction in the latter had been a quick half-hour crash course in how to play hymns for congregational singing hastily demonstrated to me by Faythe a few days before her departure. The nourishing affirmation of our loving and supportive congregation had now given me the impetus and desire to become a musician that would not only be skillful but would enable the message to minister and speak to the hearts of worshippers. I knew I had found my passion in life. Now I had to make up for such a late start in serious study! I was clueless as to how unprepared I really was in most respects.

As far back as I can remember, the wheels were always turning. Most often the main event was the annual musical in our garage "theater" at the close of each summer. My most memorable occasion, according to the local neighborhood kids, was a staging of "Sleeping Beauty" inspired by the full-length Walt Disney animated movie, which was filled with the strains of lovely Tchaikovsky melodies. I spent several weeks just gluing and painting the cardboard shingles I had created to place on the cottage home rooftop deep in the forest where the good fairies Flora, Fauna, and Merryweather were hiding Princess Aurora in order to protect her from "pricking her finger on the spindle before her twenty-first birthday." Naturally, for a director to portray this as "real," I had to include an improvised rope pulley to enable the black raven (evil Maleficent, incognito) to swoop down and discover the plot to thwart her curse upon spying the colored "fairy dust" arising from the chimney as the tiny trio of protectors argued over which color the newly designed dress of the princess would become in the end! Even Dr. Amberry, the affable, almost seven-foot-tall podiatrist, requested a detailed progress report on the "big production" at the weekly visits to his office occurring during that period.

I was age eleven when our mother's long-awaited purchase, a restored mirrored and cut-down upright piano, arrived at our small home in Lakewood, California. I was instantly taken with it. Seeing such interest, Mother took it upon herself to immediately teach me using her childhood *John M. Williams First Grade Piano* book. That was about the extent of my formal keyboard instruction as a child, since my seeming resistance to her instruction in "learning to count correctly" somewhat frustrated her. Normally very patient, she eventually found it easier to "leave me to my own devices," as there was certainly no extra cash to afford the luxury of formal lessons. Upon hearing George Gershwin's "Rhapsody in Blue" over the radio, I dreamed of one day having the ability to play this captivating piece!

The weekly string class offered to interested upper-grade children at Holmes Elementary School was always anticipated by me. I especially enjoyed the thrill of being surrounded by the colorful ensemble of sounds when we joined together with other schools to participate in the all-city orchestra concerts. Our grandfather, Walter Edward Singer, had been a professional violinist, so we had his fine instrument to use. (One time Mother shared with me that even after numerous years of not playing, he was at last coaxed to pick up his instrument. To the amazement of all, his fingers ran the scales almost effortlessly—as if he had never laid it down! Sadly, he had put aside his violin and bow permanently twenty-some years earlier in despondency over the sudden death of his young wife Agnes Drimal, a Czechoslovakian dancer. She, along with their second child, died during childbirth.)

Walter Edward Singer's history has always intrigued me because even our dad, Walter Frank Singer, knew very little regarding his father's family roots in England. The story was only that he, at age 16, along with his older brother Sidney, had abruptly left Margate, England, in the district of Kent, and sailed to the United States. Upon arriving, they entered through Ellis Island. Grandfather arrived with basically the clothes on his back and his violin! For some unknown reason, Sidney left his younger brother to survive by himself in New York City while he took off to the northwest coast!

Apparently Grandfather did find work as an instrumentalist, my dad would later recall. He would hear him rehearsing orchestra members in their living room when he was a three-year-old boy. There was always a great deal of mystery surrounding him because he would never divulge any personal information about his English family. Relatives of Agnes would insist that he came from the family of either a Duke or an Earl, but my dad knew nothing with the exception of one photo showing his Aunt Fanny standing in a beautiful rose garden. We only knew her name was Fanny because we found an old music score of "Bless This House" in his few belongings after his passing with the words: "Dear Walter with love, Sister Fanny."

We never knew Grandfather as the impeccably-dressed man pictured with his wife and infant son in our only photograph passed to us from a niece of Grandmother Agnes. The man we remember rented a room in a small Long Beach, California, home and daily wore overalls, with the exception of a simple tan jacket and dark brown dress pants reserved for Sundays and special holidays. However, he could not completely hide his privileged aristocratic upbringing. His exquisite penmanship and refined musical skills told another story—which I guess, somewhat wistfully, might not ever be known.

JUNIOR HIGH, FOR MANY, is a bit of a challenge. It was all of that and more for me! Most of my friends appeared to have shed their childhood to suddenly morph into teenagers during that brief summer vacation preceding the seventh grade. However, in most respects, I was still at heart a child who was not quite ready to suddenly discard my imaginative ways just yet. I was now keenly aware of my unusual height, and looking different was not at all what this age celebrated.

The one positive highlight for me, however, was Hoover Junior High School's orchestra! Handsome and soft-spoken Mr. Russell Latham was the instrumental musical director. He seemed to sense that I might be struggling a bit fitting into the junior high setting and was especially kind and affirming. I recall that by the eighth grade I had advanced to being third chair violin and was poised to become "concert mistress" the next year, when the ninth-graders ahead of me would be promoted on to high school. There was one upperclassman, the fourth-chair violinist, sharing my stand. Clifton Snider, son of a minister, was a more advanced player, in my opinion. I was disappointed when he decided to "challenge" for my third-chair position for the reminder of the year. The procedure was to go into a large coat closet off the rehearsal hall where Mr. Latham would hear us, sight unseen, play a short excerpt of his determination.

A few days later we were ready to proceed. I played first, followed by Clifton. I knew that Mr. Latham had to know who was playing because my able challenger had quite a large and noticeable vibrato. I did not expect to keep my seat, but when Mr. Latham chose #1, I was elated, though very surprised. I felt in my heart that this teacher was giving me some special encouragement during a diffi-cult period of childhood. I would find out years later that Clifton had been greatly admired at that time by a trea-sured friend I would meet in the future. This friend laugh-ingly confessed that she had harbored a secret "crush" on him as a teenager.

One other talented musician from this youthful orches-tra was Steve Pierson. He played the viola and seemed to know Mr. Latham quite well on a more personal level. In addition, he was then acting a bit part in the old "Donna Reed" TV series as "Zack" the paperboy. A few years later I would accidentally run into him in the music department hallway of Long Beach State College, only to learn of Mr. Latham's sad and tragic death. (Of course, I should know by now not to use any form of the word "accidental." By the time you reach the end of this saga, you will see that noth-ing much in my life can be prefaced with this adjective!)

I had the unexpected blessing of now attending a pri-vate Christian school, so I did not stay at Hoover Junior High for the ninth grade to be in orchestra as first chair— my only real regret. I have several memories of Brethren High School days that I recall with a smile. The eighth-

and ninth-grade chorus under the direction of the multi-talented and well-loved Wesley Harty was a highlight for me as a freshman. In the tenth grade I was disappointed that I could not make the cut for the elite a cappella chorus under the leadership of Carleda Hutton, an excellent musician. My high school best friend, Leana Weeks, *did* pass the auditions, so I felt even more disappointed that I could not join her. Very few in high school associated my name with music, since all the "musical" students were in choir! Although I loved to sing from childhood, as did all of my family, I could barely squeak out a note when it came to the audition day.

My mother was a very proficient singer, as were her parents. Following a voice recital as a young woman, Mother had been written up in a local newspaper as having held "great promise as a soprano." I never knew this until I found the clipping in her scrapbook following her death at age sixty-five. She had always been active as a church soloist wherever we worshipped. The last solo she sang was "In Old Judea." I was there visiting from Texas and accompanied her that December Sunday morning at my beloved childhood church. She sang with renewed energy and conviction, despite her failing strength that was beginning to ebb away due to her long battle with kidney disease.

I had one opportunity during those years at Brethren High School to play a role in one of the programs presented by the choir. It was a work entitled "The Angel Story," written and directed by the above Wesley Harty. During lunch hour one day, I attended a casting call being held for non-singing roles. The part I was hoping to secure was the tall, always tardy angel Grace, who was to play the sidekick to the very short Gloria, who was always a bit annoyed with her counterpart's habit of being late for everything. That was one part I *just knew* I could secure. After all, I was the tallest girl in the school! Even though I was typically perceived as the "quiet Marilyn Singer," I was confident that I could "get into character" due to the years of experience in my garage theater days! (And by the way, I got the part!)

I ALSO HAVE BRETHREN HIGH SCHOOL to thank for furthering my education after graduation, since no one before me in my immediate family line had done so. Brethren kept me in college prep classes all four years, and I sort of fell into college as a matter of course. I was not sure what major to pursue until one Wednesday evening after choir practice when Paul said to me, "So what are you going to major in...music?" *Music?* I thought to myself, *Why, I could major in music!* In my naivete, I had no knowledge of the necessary prerequisites that should have been met for pursuing a major in the arts. Noting the myriad music courses available at Cal State Long Beach and all that I might learn, I eagerly enrolled.

Concurrently I also enrolled as a student of music at Arlington College, our denomination's tiny school sitting at the bottom of the hill adjacent to Cal State University, Long Beach. Arlington's two-story classroom structure sat facing a similar-sized dormitory building on a couple acres of ground, the idea being that all general education and nonreligious courses were to be taken at the state school and the remaining Bible and private music instruction at Arlington. On the first day at Arlington I was introduced to Gayle Schoepf, my six-foot tall piano professor (an instant commonality!) She did not appear to be daunted when it came to taking on a student with very minimal background. Somehow this enthusiastic and positive instructor saw potential despite the awkward fingers and bad habits that would usually dictate certain failure.

At Cal State I unknowingly slipped through the educational cracks and, as a result, was accepted as a music major without ever being scheduled to audition. By the time this was discovered, I was already past the half-way point in the first semester. When I was then advised by faculty that "you can't just start college as a piano major without being somewhere around grade eight level," I did not really know what else to do but finish that first year. Gayle, back at Arlington, never seemed discouraged, and under her guidance I plugged away for the first time to master scales and arpeggios in all keys, a feat which should have already been accomplished by this point! It was Gayle who eventually helped me learn to play "Rhapsody in Blue," that childhood dream. Although technically over my head at the time, I enjoyed the challenge.

Up on the hill my Musicianship I professor, Mr. Ruger, was in contrast a somewhat ill-tempered, elderly composer who rarely cracked a smile. Upon learning of my unsuitable background, he was rather perturbed at my taking up space in his classroom at a major university. He flat out in front of the entire class stated that I would *never* be successful! When I stammered, "*Actually, I have played violin since the fourth grade*," he snapped sarcastically saying, "*Perhaps you'd better forget the piano and stick to the violin!*" With my rather innate shyness I was, of course, pretty intimidated, which ironically worked to my benefit, causing me to spend countless hours practicing cadences and singing intervals to hopefully pass and disappear gracefully from the music program.

When the day of those dreaded final exams arrived, I entered his classroom at my assigned time for the "practical" section of the exam that was to be done at the piano. Somehow I played through those numerous and varied cadences successfully in all the keys he would name and correctly recognized away from the piano the intervals that he played. For the first time ever in my presence, he suddenly smiled and nodded in affirmation saying, "Well, you just keep going on!" (Ironically, a seasoned piano teacher and I were almost the only "As" in his course that semester despite the numerous advanced musicians taking the required course—no doubt only because they felt such rudimentary work was a waste of time for them and did not prepare.) I did complete Musicianship II and Music Theory II courses during the spring semester, but only as an undeclared major so that I could at least finish out the year.

$\mathcal{M}$Y SECOND YEAR was spent only at Arlington each morning as a part-time student. I was still living at home thirty minutes from campus. Afternoons were spent at a medical assistant school near our home. (My parents and I decided that I should have some sort of practical vocation, since only a very few can readily survive on the uncertain earnings of a musician.) That spring I earned my symbolic white nurse's cap because I had mastered the bookwork. However, I could not make above a "C" in the practical applications. They granted me the diploma while privately advising that medicine was probably not the best choice for me! (Giving shots to oranges was much different than doing so to a living person, and I was much too squeamish for that!)

Jean Helbling, the daughter of a Church of God pastor, had come to Arlington from Prineville, Oregon. She was a child prodigy, along with her older sister Ruth, and came from a musical family of four sisters and one brother, who later married my youngest sister Melinda. The first time I actually heard Jean play a piano solo was one Sunday evening at our church when our pastor Alvin's brother, Fred Shackleton, came to sing a few special numbers. Fred was the vocal professor and Dean of Students at Arlington College. He was a very fine tenor. Jean was dating his equally talented son Martin, whom she eventually married. At this point I had been the church pianist for two years.

After I had finished playing for the congregational singing, I moved to a chair on the platform facing the audience to enable her to sit on the piano bench to accompany Fred. After he sang several lovely sacred art songs, he requested that Jean now play one of her classical numbers. As her fingers raced across the keys, I heard Chopin's "Fantaisie-Impromptu" for the first time. It was at that moment I finally realized what the prerequisite was for being a music major! I was in awe of such technical wizardry, at the same time wishing the floor would open up to allow me to sink below and become invisible. I wasn't sure my little church would ever feel too excited by what I would be sharing on the piano after such a performance!

The congregation was all abuzz after the service, since it had been quite an unusual evening. When the following Sunday arrived, our pastor's wife, Joanne Shackleton, handed to me a copy of "Fantaisie-Impromptu" that bore her maiden name penciled at the top of the cover. She never said a word or explained why she had this music in her possession, since I don't believe that she herself played the piano. The next fall, I was pleasantly surprised when Jean asked me if I would like to be her roommate. I moved on campus for the first time, and we had a fun year together.

As the spring semester came to a close, an unexpected merger of Arlington with the larger Azusa Pacific College (now University) about an hour north of Long Beach was announced, which meant that we as a student body would all transfer to the new campus. This would allow me to continue again as a declared music major because I was officially transferring from Arlington along with my fresh-man courses at Cal State! Jean and I continued to room together in the dorm for a second year. My piano professor at Azusa, Marsha Foxgrover, seemed pleased with the prog-ress I had made to this point and continued to encourage and expose me to the wonderful world of the master com-posers. It was unbeknownst to me then that she was the sister of Jan Sanborn, a well-known pianist and composer.

My desire at this point was to participate in the concert choir at Azusa, but my trembling "Nervous Nellie" vocal audition no doubt put others ahead of me for those cov-eted openings. It wasn't that I had never sung much, since I remember singing trios with my two sisters as soon as the youngest, Melinda, could see over the pulpit—although I was the one who always had to be closest to the micro-phone to make the equal blend. My two siblings with their lovely voices, along with our mother, were the ones that really reflected our maiden name of "Singer" of all things!

Just before the second semester began, I happened to see the distinguished, albeit slightly stern-appearing direc-tor, Professor Earle H. Anderson, walk by near the music office where I was standing. On impulse that was totally out of character for me, I hurried up to him and asked, "If anyone should drop out of concert choir, would there be any way I could take their place?" He stopped and (after quite a long pause) suddenly turned around, looked at me, and said, "Marilyn, you are in!" Then he smiled broadly and walked away.

That semester the choir took their yearly tour over spring break, going as far north as Seattle, Washington. Since I was new to the group, I was personally acquainted with only a few members. Near the beginning of the bus tour, I happened to find myself sitting across the aisle from Robert McFarland. I knew his brother Stuart from my theory class. These two young men had come from Indiana to attend this college in California because their father, Dr. James McFarland, was then head of the science department. I am not sure what prompted us to begin to chat that day except that it must have been destined.

At that time Robert did not appear to overly socialize with many of the choir members since his high school sweetheart, Margaret Cullen, was back home attending another university. As we talked casually and then more personally, we became companions the remainder of the trip. He revealed that he was a double major of Bible and music and felt called to the ministry. He also told me all about Margaret and that she would be coming there to visit on her spring break in a few weeks. He asked if she might stay in the dorm with my roommate Jean and me. As a result, I made another endearing lifelong friend, who is still an important part of my life today.

THE NEXT SUMMER I was invited to visit Noblesville, Indiana, where I met Robert's schoolteacher mother, Jane McFarland, and marveled at what she was imparting musically to those students fortunate enough to sing in her local high school choirs. (At 95 years of age at this point, she is still directing choirs of young voices—with perfect Westminster Choir College diction. She continues to teach numerous piano students and has been living in Texas even longer than we.)

While in Noblesville, I stayed with Margaret and her parents in their historical old-fashioned home. The family-owned "Grandpa's Candy Shop" was still in operation sitting beside the road at the front of their property. I loved meeting the Cullens! I am afraid they found me a bit unforgettable, since my improperly placed upstairs shower curtain allowed water to flood their antique living room below! (A few years later, my "favor" was repaid when Margaret's sister Jane stayed with us one night in Santa Ana: the not-yet-caulked guest bath upstairs did the same to our living room ceiling!)

During that same visit, I almost stepped foot on a Tom Sawyer-inspired wooden raft to cruise down the White River. At the last minute, the makeshift engine suddenly caught fire and ended a several-week project that Robert and his friends had built during summer break. I also traveled deep into the Georgian woods to hear Robert's grandfather, an old-fashioned Methodist Evangelist, Reverend Harry Blackburn, while experiencing both horseflies and camp meeting for the first and only time. To and from that destination, I enjoyed a sweet time of conversation with Jane McFarland as she and I traveled along a route that revealed the aftermath of a recent hurricane.

That following fall semester, Robert brought with him not only Margaret but his fellow "Tom Sawyerites" as well, having themselves been former high school members of Jane McFarland's dynamic choral group. We were all in concert choir together, and we lived in the adjunct hillside dormitories several miles north of the main campus. Previously this property had been filled with boys from a former military school. It felt more like a mountain camp, and we loved the outdoor feeling. When the smog was not hanging over the area, the view was fantastic! Margaret and I became roommates. Our room, though old, was spacious—unlike the small and modern dorm I had shared with Jean on the main campus. (Jean was now married to Martin Shackleton and living off campus.) That was such a fun year for me to experience a more typical college life while enjoying the camaraderie of these students. I still have flashbacks of being bounced around in the back of Robert's Opel Kadett. If you (like me) were prone to becoming carsick, that was the perfect setting in which to experience it!

One memorable evening Margaret and I always laugh about was the night we impulsively decided to make a quick late-night run to a nearby burger establishment. Our room was in a tree-covered location on the very top of the sprawling dormitory complex that stretched from the bottom to the very top of a steep hill. We could come and go rather freely from our room since there were literally hundreds of stairs to climb from the location of the front dorm mother's desk on the ground floor to our residence at the topmost room on the top floor. Conveniently, there was a door providing easy access to the outside and the upper parking lot. That night, after already dressed for bed, we donned our raincoats over our nightgowns and ventured out in Robert's car. I was in the front seat this time, thank goodness! We pulled in and proceeded to the drive-through window (we thought very discretely). As we were pulling away, the young man who took our order called after us saying, "Do you always visit the In-N-Out Burger in your nightgowns?" Somehow he had caught a glimpse of our unusual evening attire!

That same semester, the pool of available pianists was rather low when I learned that Mr. Anderson was desperate for an accompanist. Of course, my former roommate Jean would have been his first choice. However, she was on a scholarship that required playing for the college's traveling ensemble, the Dynamics Chorale. I remember Mr. Anderson asking her in my presence if she thought I could handle the job. She nodded slightly, no doubt put on the spot. (I am not sure he was totally reassured by such over-enthusiasm, but I got the job!)

Mr. Anderson proved to be a deeply sensitive conductor. He eventually seemed not always as intimidating as he could appear when his bushy eyebrows were knit together and intensely focused on interpreting a score! He was a fine baritone and deeply committed to excellence in conveying through music the message of Christ. In addition, he taught private voice and directed the oratorio chorus (my first introduction to Mendelssohn's dramatic Elijah!) as well as the opera workshop. Professor Anderson had previously been a performer with the Los Angeles Opera Company.

I still remember quite vividly the first college chapel service for which the choir sang when I began my role as accompanist. I was pretty nervous. To make matters worse, our first number began with a highly articulated sixteenth-note introduction for Eugene Butler's rousing anthem "How Excellent is Thy Name!" Professor Anderson gave the downbeat and I literally froze. Undeterred, he gave it again with no response. Then in a loud irritated whisper he shouted: "*Marilyn!*" Needless to say, I finally got going!

Young Robert McFarland, even at age eighteen, could sing anyone "under the table" with his rich and mature baritone voice. It was he who encouraged me probably more than any other person at Azusa Pacific and provided many opportunities to learn and interpret vocal accompaniments that were technically somewhat above my head. The one thing I admit I must have had going for me was the extraordinary passion and love for anything musical or creative. I seemed to desire to "soak it all in like a sponge" whenever, wherever, and from whomever!

When Robert and his future bride Margaret were preparing for her senior recital, which they were planning to do jointly, the music chosen had very challenging accompaniments. Mr. Anderson was a little concerned that this might be too difficult for me, but Robert was insistent that I be their pianist. (Now that is a die-hard friend!) Eventually, Mr. Anderson acquiesced and allowed me to do it. Robert spent countless hours working with me in the practice room to perfect musical interpretations and tempos, and I sure did practice! I was ecstatic when Mr. Anderson seemed genuinely pleased with the results. Robert later went on to become a renowned international operatic baritone after winning the Metropolitan Opera auditions. Soon afterward he began his opera career in the New York City Opera under Beverly Sills, and he eventually had the privilege of singing with all of the "Three Tenors" over his long career!

ANOTHER SIGNIFICANT RECOLLECTION from the Azusa days was a recital I attended on campus. As music majors, we were all required to attend a certain number of recitals each semester. On that particular evening, I was tired and tempted to just skip this one. I had never heard the names Robert Hale, a baritone, and Ovid Young, his accompanist, the guest artists who were performing that night. Paul Lundberg, one of Azusa Pacific's music faculty, had arranged for this particular program, as I recall. At the last minute, I decided to attend. When I heard the performance of these two artists together, it was a life-changing moment. Never before had I heard such singing and playing, and I decided that evening *this* was the kind of music I wanted to be able to do well. Ovid Young was already a published arranger, and I began to seek out any music that bore his name because it was always so expressive and creative. Music in the church was starting to change. Even as a young adult, I found it difficult to embrace much of the new contemporary trend. The words and music just did not speak as profoundly to my heart and soul in this genre.

The last year I attended Azusa, the concert choir experienced a memorable trip to Jerusalem to sing at a national convention on biblical prophecy. While at that conference, I remember hearing the powerful music of Jerome Hines.

(At that time, I was unaware of his esteemed reputation in the opera world.) After one of the services, Jean and I wandered about backstage until we found Mr. Hines in an empty room. I don't remember any conversation with him, but he did pose for what proved to be a dark and rather poorly focused picture when the film was eventually developed.

The choir was housed at the Mount of Olives Hotel in the Arab section of the city. At first the men who served at the hotel were a bit standoffish and probably not keen on having this group from the United States in their midst. However, when a week had passed, they prepared for us their version of an "American" meal and actually had tears in their eyes when our bus rolled away to travel into Europe for the next part of our journey.

One day before leaving Jerusalem, I remember a conversation that three of us were having after lunch. We were talking about what we would do following graduation. My friends, both quite accomplished musicians, were stating that they would probably pursue getting their master's degrees. I mentioned that I had wondered if I should do the same. Half in jest, one of them said, "Well, some girls should probably just think about getting their 'M-R-S' degree, since everyone is *not* graduate material!"

$\mathcal{A}$S IT TURNED OUT, I didn't have to worry about making that big decision. Soon after I met my "prince charming," Bill Thompson, and was married the following year. As you will later learn when this part of the story unfolds, Bill was indeed closely linked to American "royalty" (of sorts!).

After becoming engaged, I decided to pursue the purchase of a small grand piano. Up until this time, I would always drive the twenty minutes from my parents' home to practice on the small Yamaha grand in the sanctuary of our church. It seemed at the time such a luxury to play when compared to our old upright that had been my only real practice instrument since graduation from college. I had saved enough for a small down payment on a new Kawai I had searched out at the local music store. The $2,100 price tag was way out of my reach, but I thought that this purchase would also be a means of establishing credit. Wow, what a happy surprise and wedding gift to learn that my husband-to-be had later gone in and paid the bill in full a couple of weeks before our wedding! Now I had a quality *grand* piano of my own!

Our special day was a memorable occasion of rainbow sherbet colors—what else would blend with avocado green carpet? Of course, we had lots of wonderful music provided by friends. Jean played the piano and Marsha Foxgrover played the organ. (Although the Conn organ was a new and appreciated addition to our little church, it definitely was not an organist's dream instrument!) I paid for most of my wedding dress by giving my friend Sharon Stiles' husband Jerry piano lessons over the next year or so! This wedding was done on a very tiny shoestring budget helped by $200 in an envelope that unexpectedly appeared in my parents' mailbox from a family on an American base in Germany.

Two years prior, during the college choir tour, we had a performance on an army base for a Sunday service. Before the bus departed from the base, a lady was seen outside speaking with Professor Anderson. After our director got on board, he walked back to my seat and handed me an envelope that contained $150. Apparently the lady requested that he give it to a student in need and was given my name. She also told him that if she ever felt led at some future time to help me, she might send more. Mr. Anderson knew of my mother's rare illness and the resulting financial hardships of my dad working to establish his struggling custom gear manufacturing business while also taking care of my mother. I was so grateful for the gift, since I was on this trip with very little cash to spend for anything.

The night of the wedding, the small church was filled. That Saturday evening was one of the warmest on record for Southern California. Those unfortunate souls forced to sit in the balcony said they sweltered (no air-conditioning then) while the neighbor's dog barked incessantly. Of course, I never noticed! My cousin tells me that the sherbet punch had been diluted to pure water by the time he came through the reception line. The entire church had been invited, and I did not have anyone to really advise me on preparing for such a large crowd. Mother had been ill for almost a decade and was barely able to be in attendance. (A year later, she had a miraculous remission of her rare and incurable nephrotic syndrome and was restored to good health for another twelve years, which allowed her to welcome the birth of her grandchildren and enjoy an active part in their early childhood. Eventually dialysis treatments became necessary the last four to five years of her life. However, unlike most patients, she could drive herself three times a week to the hospital since she felt no sickness or any of the usual discomforts that most in her situation experience.)

The first Christmas following our marriage, I flew to Seattle with Bill to join his mother and family and be introduced to additional family members and friends for the first time. Unfortunately for me, I was "celebrating" the second month of pregnancy "morning sickness" that was actually pretty much unrelenting day and night! Despite my queasy stomach, I still enjoyed the lovely week with these dear people.

In my earlier reference to Bill being related to American "royalty": His cousin David Abbot (Bud) on his mother's side lived in the original mansion known as the Duthe House, built by shipbuilder John F. Duthe in the early 1900's and subsequently remodeled by William E. Boeing in 1942 when he took possession.

Sitting farther up the hill was now the newer home of the aircraft giant. David, as had his father "Dutch" before him, managed the large Boeing ranch. Known now as Aldarra Farms, it was set in the picturesque hills of Fall City, Washington. Bud's tradition each year was to cut down one of the 10' tall stately pine trees surrounding the perimeter of the property and stand it from floor to ceiling in the entryway, encircled by the home's grand wooden spiral staircase. Being a traditionalist overall by nature, I remember wondering how Mr. Boeing would now prefer the square, rather cold modernistic structure he had built to such an earlier vintage residence. However, it was definitely a generous perk for his ranch manager to enjoy for many years as part of his salary! I was struck by Bud's genteel and quiet nature, which was totally unlike the rough and tumble kind of personality I would have expected in his profession!

Several months after our marriage, I became friends with Janice Roush Wood, a quick-witted and fun young woman who became the wife of our music director, Paul. She was a skilled keyboardist, and we enjoyed playing piano and organ duets as young adults. We quickly became close and remained so for many years until an untimely brain tumor claimed her life. I will never forget the lovely poetry and lyrics she was gifted at writing.

On one occasion, Janice and I had put together our own Christmas concert, where I remember trying my inexperienced hand at a couple of piano-organ arrangements. They were probably not too intricate or profound, but I do remember enjoying this first real attempt at creative writing. (During this performance, firstborn infant Melody made her presence known from the nursery adjoining the small sanctuary!) Unexpectedly, a sweet lady in our congregation named Helen Barkley, known for her lovely singing abilities, walked up to me afterward. She was most sincere in her encouragement and appreciation of the arrangements.

Many years and many miles passed. Naturally, I was quite surprised to run into Helen Barkley, now in Oklahoma City some thirty-plus years later. She was singing along with our daughter in their church choir! (Also, Helen's niece in Oklahoma had become close friends with our Melody.) This incident has reminded me of how a simple caring word of encouragement to another person can put a smile on their face and validity to their endeavors, even if it does not measure up to our "standards" or self-perceived abilities at the time. I so desire to always be that kind of person! Helen passed away several years later, but the comforting memory of her lives on always in my heart whenever she comes to mind.

BILL AND I were living in our first home in Huntington Beach, California, while I was enjoying being a mother to our firstborn, Melody. I continued to play for the church and taught piano to a handful of children from the neighborhood. One day Mr. L. D. Thomas came by to tune our piano. As we were casually chatting, I told him that I would really like to find a teacher and continue my studies at home. "Oh," he said almost immediately, "you need to see Mr. Robert Dick in nearby Costa Mesa and learn about the Trinity College of Music program based in London, England." It was not too long after that conversation I decided to study with Mr. Dick, and I worked through the Associate and Licentiate Degrees in teaching with the assistance of this fine teacher. Mother offered to come each week to babysit and enjoy her first grandchild to make this study possible for me.

Soon after I began my Trinity studies, I met the young woman who took the lesson before mine. Mr. Dick suggested we perform a two-piano number together for an upcoming Christmas student recital. Marilyn Kunde, daughter of a minister, is a lovely blond of Scandinavian roots. She played for a large church in Costa Mesa that was associated with Southern California College (now Vanguard University). Marilyn had a beautiful style of playing and as a teenager had been the star pupil of Mary Jean Brown, a well-known pianist and teacher in the area. She also enjoyed creating hymn arrangements for piano. Marilyn's smile was as big as her heart!

I was expecting our second child, Mark, at the time. Although I was continually fighting morning sickness twenty-four hours a day, I invited her to lunch one afternoon to become better acquainted, since she lived just a few miles away from us in Westminster. She jokes that this was the first time she ever had an avocado sandwich!

To this day she is like a true member of our remaining family. She was so burdened with the plight of the poor and needy that she basically set aside her own goals in music and began a ministry that has aided many who have seemingly been forgotten around the world. Love-Lift Ministries is her life! She and her late husband Philip had traveled many miles at their own expense to deliver basic living supplies, quilts, and little surprises to light up the eyes of those who have nothing in the way of worldly goods. One memory I have of Marilyn always makes me giggle. Whenever she was introduced to someone in my presence, she was sure to add the following additional facts: "We had so much in common because we both played piano and loved doing hymn arrangements, we both played violin, and we both married 'older' husbands!" She always made sure to include *all* of the above!

In the midst of my Trinity studies, we moved to Santa Ana and away from Huntington Beach, the windy weather, and the usual damp and overcast mornings. Before the ministry became a full-time responsibility, Marilyn Kunde used to participate in a string group that practiced in Garden Grove on Thursday evenings. After her rehearsal, she would stop by for an hour or so to visit since she was in the nearby vicinity. During that time she shared many of the improvisational ideas she had learned from Mary Jean Brown. I usually had prepared brownies or some type of dessert for us to snack on. Most of the little musical decorations that are displayed in our home came from Marilyn Kunde, as she has never forgotten a birthday or special occasion in over forty-five years of friendship. She, her husband Philip, and their son Christopher are like our own family. I would certainly be remiss if I did not express appreciation for their positive impact on our entire family.

The final step in my Trinity College of Music education was the Fellows Diploma that would be earned only after passing an extensive theory examination coupled with a successful full piano recital for the examiners sent from London to adjudicate. It was usually in the spring that they came to the California center, hosted by Robert Dick, himself a Fellow of Trinity.

OUR FRIENDS Janice and Paul Shackleton were now attending First Church of the Nazarene, having felt the desire to be in a larger congregation. We had been feeling for some time the need for fellowship and support of other young adults, which was important for our growing family. The Shackletons encouraged us to visit their new church home.

The summer in July just prior to our considering a decision to leave our little church, I had given my first formal piano recital in the sanctuary. The first half of the program consisted of a few classical solos. My Arlington professor, Gayle, had agreed to come and share in this performance. She played several organ solos, and then we played Ravel's "Pavane for a Dead Princess." The program concluded with my second attempts at hymn arrangements for sacred piano-organ duets. These pieces, "Variations on Greensleeves" and "Praise to the Lord, the Almighty," are still among my favorites today.

Mr. Dick was present for this recital. I was far from perfect, but it was a great accomplishment for me to have played such a program nonetheless. I remember that Marilyn Kunde was also in attendance and came up to me afterward with a gift of a lovely set of decorated tiles of Chopin and Mozart. I still have these displayed on my sheet music cabinet. She has always been among the most giving and thoughtful friends that I have ever known, even in those early years of getting acquainted. The next month, August, I had requested some vacation time from my church responsibilities. I had been there ten years without much time off and needed a break. Life was pretty busy with our two young children. We decided to visit the Nazarene Church and see if God was leading in this direction.

At the same time, our current church was interviewing Janet and Dayle Wilson as candidates for the now-open position of minister of music. The young couple was Jean Helbling Shackleton's sister and brother-in-law. I was asked during my vacation to attend the Tuesday night church council meeting to sit in on their interview. I don't remember all that was discussed except that Dayle made the statement: "When I come as minister of music, I always have my wife as the accompanist." I was caught off guard slightly, as I thought it unusual he would have been so adamant about it with me sitting right across the table from him. Of course, I realized that Janet was probably very accomplished, being the sister of Jean. Pastor Shackleton with his kindly and soft-spoken humor said, "Well, Marilyn just gave us a concert. Wait 'til you hear her. You will want to use them both!" There was no response from Dayle, and the meeting progressed quickly to an end. It was unanimously decided that Dayle and Janet would come the next month.

It was at this moment I determined in my heart I would never answer a call for service if it required overshadowing or replacing any person who was fulfilling a personal ministry calling on their life. It might have been very demoralizing if we had not already felt the desire in our hearts to move on in order to meet our family needs. As I left that evening, I knew it was time for us to follow God's prompting. I was happy the church would not be left lacking in any way.

My last Sunday at this church was the week before Janet and Dayle's arrival. Unexpectedly, the service came and went without any announcement to the congregation that this was to be our last day. It was painful for me not to be able to say a formal goodbye to the many I loved dearly or to tell them why we felt God was moving us into a new chapter of our lives. Mother cried that day, and so did I. I guess deep down our dear pastor did not want to accept that we were really going. I know he grieved the loss of his son Paul as music director a year prior, and now we were also leaving. Sadly, I don't think he ever fully understood the reasons until a number of years had passed.

Later that same week, Pastor Shackleton called and said that he had a book the church wanted to give me. He offered to bring it over. I told him, "No, I would much prefer to come to the next service and receive it so that I could share a few words." I am not sure whether or not he wanted me to do this, but after hesitating he agreed. It was awkward, but I felt it was important to speak to my church family to let them know that I was not leaving the treasured relationships of my youth easily. I could not bear to just disappear without an explanation.

With little fanfare or lofty words of farewell, a lovely collection of inspirational writings was presented to me. It was months before I could open it. When I finally did, one choir member had written, "Your place is still here; come fill it!" At that particular time, the age demographics of the church made it difficult for them to understand our changing needs as a family. I can truly understand this to a certain degree. At times an individual can find it difficult to celebrate someone else moving on if one feels it leaves a void in their own life.

Not too long after we left, however, Mother began to play the organ at the church. She and Janet developed a close relationship as they ministered together. Mother enjoyed this opportunity so much that she began studying organ at the local junior college to improve her skills. She and Dad found and purchased an exact replica of the little Conn church organ for sale in a local classified ad. She could practice at home now without having to make the thirty-minute trips to the church. She continued to serve faithfully for many years, even when her health began to decline.

As for me, I would spend almost a year grieving inside for the loss and wondering if this new church would ever feel like home. Looking back, however, if we had not made the move, I would never have known the people who would soon impact my life rather dramatically in several new directions.

Soon I HAD THE OPPORTUNITY to assume the position of choir accompanist under Steve Brown at First Church of the Nazarene. His heart was as huge as his baritone voice. He introduced us all to *Amahl and the Night Visitors,* and our two eldest children, even at ages three and five, were totally enthralled! (Our third child, Melissa, came along two years later.) We performed that beloved opera several times, and it remains a favorite to this day.

I will never forget the awesome nine-foot Steinway in the large sanctuary that played like a dream. (The famous pianist Roger Williams offered to buy it for many times the cost—it was *that* wonderful!) There was also the Christmas occasion we had the ultimate luxury of three such pianos sitting in our sanctuary—and they were all playing their own individual parts undergirded with the huge, resonant sounds of the organ! I was stunned as the congregation applauded and spontaneously arose from their seats, almost as one, in a joyous response of praise to God that Sunday morning.

The late Albert Skiles and Dwane Prescott shared the duties of the finest Allen organ of the day. Also among this congenial and dedicated group of talented musicians was an elegant lady, Charlotte Herrick, who was both a highly accomplished soprano soloist and a pianist. I am eternally grateful for the many classical and sacred concerts that were presented and received so warmly at Santa Ana First Church of the Nazarene. I still remember this period as being among the most fulfilling times in my life for making music. We all loved and cheered each other on without any feelings of competition. It was a true ministry in every respect.

Strings have always been my favorite orchestral instruments. Dan Choi, a young man and very skilled violinist, became active in our congregation. There was also a teen girl named Angie Holscher who was studying violin in school, as well as Janice Duerksen, about my age, who was pretty much a beginner on the cello. The one thing we lacked for a quartet was a viola player. After searching the local classifieds, I found a viola, case, and bow listed for eighty dollars. That same evening I made an appointment to meet the man who was selling it. I ended up buying it—not really knowing anything about what I should be looking for in this instrument. However, it did have a lovely tone. After mastering that pesky alto clef, we could now have a real quartet!

I enjoyed the viola due to its larger size and because I loved playing the inner harmonies that are often the "bread and butter" of the violist. On occasion, Marilyn Kunde would join us with her violin. We had the best time and actually sounded fairly good for such a diverse group, making it a nice addition on an occasional Sunday. A number of years later I would have the opportunity in several congregations to form other such groups. Surprisingly, I did find out years later that my rather spontaneous purchase was actually a fine German viola, and I still enjoy playing it today!

During those ten years in that positive setting, a number of lasting friendships were made. Mr. L. Harold Johnston, who for many years had used his musical skills in that very church, had a tender heart for God and was loved by all who knew him. He shared many of his creative improvisational ideas with me and was a sensitive interpreter of all styles of music. (Even in his nineties, this kindly

gentlemen continued to minister on the keyboard at the Ridgecrest Church of the Nazarene in California. He resided in Ridgecrest until his death on Father's Day in 2017.)

One recollection I hold in particular of Harold Johnston involves an old cast-off upright piano one of his food service customers had sitting in a covered patio next to a swimming pool of all places! This customer had offered it free to Harold as a useful way to develop the skills he was attempting to master in a Saturday course on piano tuning and repair at a local junior college.

I had recently expressed to him my desire to provide a piano for my musical sister and brother-in-law so that their two young children could have piano lessons. Money was very tight for them, and such a costly instrument was not at all in their budget. We came up with the bright idea that the above-mentioned instrument might be the answer!

With Bill's permission, the piano was hauled to our garage to be worked on by Harold when his work schedule permitted. Well, that did not happen too often, so Ken Churchill, the college instructor, invited me to sit in on the

Saturday classes for the remaining weeks of the current fall semester so that I could assist—since the idea was to have this ready by Christmas!

Of course, neither one of us knew what we were getting into! Ken handed me a box full of old keys and hammers and showed me what to do to replace and glue all the non-working parts. My parents even got into the act. Dad made a brand-new top to replace the one that was half decayed from being stored next to water. Mother helped me to strip off the old green paint covering the once-beautifully stained mahogany case. The big question on everyone's mind was "would these 'bones' live?"

Finally, the parts were together. Ken took pity on us and came over to "regulate" the hammers (i.e., get some sound out of it)! Somehow tones actually resounded from the instrument! I put a huge bow on the "PSO" (piano-shaped object, a term I later gleaned from my future mentor) and presented it to my sister and family with joy and tears of happiness that made it worth every hour of labor and learning!

A second rather poignant remembrance of Harold involved our piano/organ duet, "The Hiding Place." When Bill and I were dating, we had gone to see the same-named movie depicting the Dutch watchmaker and Christian, Cornelia Arnolda Johanna "Corrie" Ten Boom—who, along with her father and other family members, helped many Jews escape the Nazi Holocaust during World War II by hiding them in her closet. She was later imprisoned in the Ravensbruck Concentration Camp.

The film had been so deeply moving to me—made even more so by the hauntingly beautiful theme song. I had not forgotten it in the five or six years since my first hearing. I felt impressed to use this theme and interweave an old favorite hymn around it. (Almost without thinking, the song that came to mind was "I Have Found a Hiding Place." I earlier referenced this same song and my simply chorded accompaniment when new to our youth group—before being "drafted" the unlikely, ill-prepared replacement for the former pianist.) I enlisted the help of Harold, and we arranged it using Tedd Smith's melody as the inspiration.

A few Sundays later, we played it together. At that time Corrie was now in failing health, living in Placentia, California, a nearby city. As I recall, neither Harold nor I were aware that one of her hospice nurses, Betsy Chappel, attended our Santa Ana church from time to time when her schedule permitted. On that particular morning, she was present in the congregation. She came up to Harold after the service all smiles and excitedly requested a cassette tape of the instrumental duet. She planned to play it for Corrie that very evening! I remember that Sunday as if it were just yesterday!

IT WAS DURING THE FIRST SEVERAL YEARS at Santa Ana First Church of the Nazarene that I made an initial attempt to gain my Fellowship Diploma through Trinity College of Music, London, England. Unfortunately, my musical interpretations were not quite convincing enough to pass the first time. I was determined to try again and prepare more thoroughly.

One evening a few months later, Dr. Michael Martin, pianist and son of a well-known Nazarene evangelist, presented a marvelous classical recital. Members of his family attended the church. He was a professor of piano at nearby Chapman University. My friend Charlotte knew him and took me to talk with him after his performance and inquire as to whether he might be willing to help me on my second attempt at receiving the Fellowship Diploma. We no longer lived close enough to Costa Mesa for me to travel as often for lessons with Robert Dick. Dr. Martin kindly offered to come to our home every week at 2:00 p.m., since he lived just a mile down the road. This was a perfect arrangement for me with my young children.

Those five to six years with Dr. Martin completely changed how my ears heard music, since he let nothing slip by that he felt was not a persuasive musical interpretation. Sometimes we might spend over an hour on just one page of music! Happily, I passed on my second attempt at a Fellowship Diploma! One of the pieces, the "Scherzo in Bb minor, Op. 31" by Chopin, became a favorite, and I performed it one evening in our church soon after I received my diploma. Jeff Moore, son of singer Gary Moore, was the music director at the time, and he insisted that I share this number with our congregation for performance experience, despite my reluctance to do so. (I have never really aspired to being a soloist and would much rather work together with others.)

Being unaware that our time in California was going to come to a close a year later, we reluctantly left our homey Cape Cod-style house in historic Santa Ana to move several miles east into the Tustin school district known for the high quality of their education. Our new house was a "fixer"—as would become our pattern of future home purchases! The beautiful yard and flowers that had drawn us in as buyers had gone to seed in the four months it took for the sale to become final. The first weekend we moved into this house we discovered that the large addition across the back of the home had nothing but thin paneling covering the studs. It took a lot of engineering to even mount a curtain rod with much security. Being that it was summer, the lack of insulation made the heat unbearable. We were stuck for sure. That winter the first rainstorm produced fifteen to twenty leaks due to the improperly designed flat roof! I still remember frantically running and grabbing every available pot or pan to catch the water drops! Somehow we survived and got it all together after many visits to Home Depot, and we were able to transform it into a very pleasant place to live.

One summer evening Ovid Young and his wife Laura were in town during a concert tour in Orange County, California. We, along with two other couples from our church, were invited to a dinner for the Youngs hosted by Dr. James and Charlotte Herrick at their home. I still recall that the meal was one of the most elegant and delicious I have ever been served. It was true to form to everything this gracious lady would ever set her hand to do! I asked for all the recipes! I do not remember participating much in the conversation and felt privileged just to be there! Following the dinner, Charlotte asked Ovid to play a number, and he immediately asked her to sing to his accompaniment. "I Will Not Forget Thee" was an expressive and beautifully rendered arrangement of an old hymn that was then new to me as a young adult. Their impromptu living room performance transformed a simple song of faith into a work of art.

After those first six months of settling into our latest abode, I had asked a man in our church, Keith, for some decorating ideas. He and his wife owned a little business and enjoyed perusing flea markets in search of interesting and inexpensive accessories for their customers. One day Keith appeared at our door with a rush-bottom chair and a tall, rather heart-shaped back. He thought we might use it in the "library," as we were calling the space, since it was lined with many bookshelves. The chair was an interesting piece of eclectic ambience to place in that room. I was delighted with his find, and the price was right—only ten dollars! What a deal! (I had no idea the impact that this chair would represent in the not-too-distant future!) Although there have been similar ones in appearance, I was never able to locate any exact matches after many online searches.

As soon as our above-mentioned home was at last ready to be enjoyed, we found ourselves packed once again—this time in preparation for the long drive to Texas, as my husband Bill had been relocated in his work. The thought of living in another state had never really crossed my mind, as I was born and raised in Southern California. It was difficult to leave my mother and dad, since Mother's health was beginning to decline. She died within a year and was never able to come to visit us in our new surroundings. Her twenty-five years of fluctuating health made a lasting impression as to how compassionate and caring a person our dad was and the depth of his love for our mother. None of us will ever forget the positive lasting legacy he left behind.

The first Sunday after moving into our new home in Fairview, Texas, we decided to visit the Richardson Church of the Nazarene. We had been in the Santa Ana First Church of the Nazarene for ten years and had loved the congregation there so much. Lifetime friends were born out of that association, so it was natural that we felt the desire to continue as we had in another Nazarene church in Texas. As was their custom, new visitors were asked to stand, and they were each given a loaf of homemade bread to welcome them that day.

After the service we began to walk toward our car when a tall, familiar-looking gentleman came striding toward us, offering his hand while saying, "Hi, my name is Ovid Young. Would you like to come to our home next Friday night for dinner?" Of course, we were delighted to accept! Charlotte Herrick, the aforementioned special musician friend from our Santa Ana church, had taken me with her on numerous occasions to the magnificent concerts that Mr. Young and the dazzling operatic singers Hale and Wilder performed every summer. Southern California was quite often on their tour agenda. She knew these fine men since college days. In addition, she introduced me to the unparalleled duo piano concerts performed by Nielson and Young that through the years had been my inspiration and example of excellence few ever attain. Hearing the sacred hymns and songs of faith garbed in such exquisite settings had a most profound influence on me as a church musician and ultimately as a composer. A year later, when Charlotte found out we were moving away, she had thoughtfully written ahead to her friends, the Youngs, to be on the look-out for us!

My husband was still to make a few trips back to California to complete the move, so our children and I were without him on that first visit to the Youngs in Carrollton. When we walked into their lovely home, something seemed vaguely familiar to me as we sat down to enjoy the wonderful lasagna that Laura had prepared. In the course of our casual "getting to know each other" conversation, we discussed their dining room table. They mentioned how they had found this set in an antique store but that there was only one thing wrong—it was missing one chair! Then I knew why there was something familiar! Suddenly I blurted out, "I think I have the missing chair…and it has traveled all these many miles from California!"

And so it was—a perfect match! The next time I came to visit I had my chair in hand. We all shook our heads in disbelief! How could this be? Ovid then left the room and carried out an unusual little piece of furniture: it folded together and then opened to reveal what appeared to be a place to sit. It was ornately carved. Someone had stripped the finish off, and it needed to be restained. "Here," he said, "take this, as we probably will never get around to restoring it, and you might enjoy this project."

I was delighted to have this unique item. I am not sure if Ovid or Laura even knew what name to give this interesting chair. *Probably* (I thought) *it needs a thick material attached in some way so one could sit on it…sort of like a portable director's chair for a movie set.* I always intended to follow through with this restoration and find the perfect spot for it. To my dismay, I never did. But this treasure traveled from house to house (in more moves than I care to admit), and it always seemed to find a special residence in the attic!

$\mathcal{A}$BOUT SIX MONTHS LATER we were feeling more at home and enjoying the small-town setting. Bill was busy and content in his job with Rockwell in Richardson, and we were still attending the large Richardson Church of the Nazarene. As time went on, however, we found the long drive down Interstate 75 to Richardson a bit tedious due to major roadwork and the resulting traffic jams. We decided then to look closer to home for a church where our family could all participate and meet friends in our neighborhood.

We kept in touch with the Youngs, however, and one Friday evening we invited them over for a meal. After dinner, Ovid asked me casually what I was working on in composition. He knew that Lillenas, the Nazarene Publishing House, and his former Olivet Nazarene University organ student, Lyndell Leatherman, had accepted my first manuscripts—even in their handwritten, penciled stage! (I learned later that Ovid had placed a call to Lyndell asking about this music after I had excitedly informed him of this good news one Wednesday evening while we were still attending the Richardson church.) These were hymn arrangements for my books entitled *Piano Worshi*p and *Heavenly Father, King Eternal,* some of which I had collaborated on with L. Harold Johnston. Rather hesitantly, I brought out my current notebook of creative efforts.

I had begun working on some duo piano numbers after we started attending the little Grace Evangelical Free Church in nearby Allen, Texas, where I met a fine musician named Linda Ash, the church pianist. We began playing together when our neighbor and friend, Rae Williamsen, also of that church, offered to store her mother's unused grand at Grace so that we could have two pianos! (At least we had a spinet and Rae's grand. This was not exactly ideal, but it was a much better match than the current small Hammond B3 organ—which I admit is still considered a "keeper" to many in pop music!)

Bill's mother Florence had passed away just before we moved from California. A few months after I began playing with Linda, a "certificate of deposit" became due that had been inherited by Bill from his mother. After having a discussion with Bill, a coworker (bless that unnamed man!) suggested that it would be a much better investment on this money to purchase a Steinway piano! I had never even considered owning such a fine instrument—so I was excited to say the least. However, when Bill and I visited the Dallas music stores, the prices quickly brought us to reality! Also, I could never find an action that duplicated the dream Steinway from the Santa Ana First Church days. Then one day Bill, who had been occasionally reading the classifieds in the Dallas Morning News, spotted an ad for a seven-foot Steinway for twelve thousand dollars—which, of course, was an unheard of price. We made the drive into Dallas to check it out. The seller was hoping to use the money from the sale to invest in electronic keyboards for her music gigs. The moment I sat down to touch the keys,

I instantly remembered the magnificent one-of-a-kind Steinway from the past! This piano was from the twenties at the height of Steinway pianos—a real find! Not only that, Bill offered her just ten thousand dollars. She took it without hesitation. This was a true gift from heaven to me!

So, my Kawai grand was loaned to the little Grace Church. What a luxury! Linda and I devoured all the wonderful Nielson and Young repertoire available at the time. I continued my efforts in creating new arrangements out of necessity for more pieces. We so enjoyed collaborating together, and the congregation seemed to love it. We also had the experience of performing a benefit duo piano concert to raise money for the Allen Outreach Center that aided those who found themselves needing assistance. The Dallas Youth Orchestra Wind Ensemble graciously assisted us on that occasion.

Now, getting back to that evening after dinner, Dr. Young opened my notebook and thumbed through a few pages. He suddenly paused when he came to my ending of the hymn arrangement "Holy, Holy, Holy" and suggested, "What might work nicely on this ending would perhaps be to use 'augmentation'" (in other words, increase the note values to elongate the timing). "Yes," I agreed nodding, "I like that idea!" About thirty minutes or so later, as the four of us were casually visiting, I asked Ovid (just to make conversation) if he taught students. "No," he replied, "but Stephen has quite a few students…however, I would be happy to take you as a student of composition." I could hardly believe what my ears had heard, since I would never have dreamed to ask this esteemed musician for any kind of lesson—let alone composition! "Oh, yes, I would love to do that!"

I was nowhere even close to Ovid's musical achievement. I had been toying with the idea of going to the University of North Texas to study on a graduate level. However, my first priority was raising our family, and the long drive and commitment did not seem like a wise choice at the time, even though I had completed the enrollment process and the majority of preliminary testing requirements.

As we eventually made our way into the living room for more conversation, Ovid asked me to play something. Of course my fingers turned to jelly, and it was the last thing I wanted to do in front of him! I could think of no gracious way to wiggle out if it. As I slowly made my way to our piano, I sighed saying, "Wow, nothing like having to play for *Beethoven*!" "No," he joked, "Beethoven is right behind you!" while casting a glance toward the plaster statue prominently displayed on top of my music cabinet in the corner of the room. Somehow I managed to wade through "Thou Didst Leave Thy Throne," the piano arrangement in my first Lillenas solo book, *Piano Worship*, dedicated to him. It was not my most relaxed performance, but evidently it was not a "deal breaker" in regard to his earlier offer of tutelage.

ND SO IT WAS that now I was in Texas all these many years later and about to drive the forty-five minutes to Carrollton to study with Dr. Ovid Young! Not long after our move from California, Robert McFarland had begun talking about recording and creating orchestrations for a hymn CD of the vocal music that Mr. L. Harold Johnston and I had arranged for him. With the advent of MIDI, the simulated "symphony orchestra" and more sophisticated software transcription programs were coming into their own. Aided by such tools, I purposed to create a soundtrack for this next phase of the project.

On my first lesson I brought Ovid an early arrangement of "I'd Rather Have Jesus" (the first selection for the subsequent McFarland CD entitled *Stormy Winds*). It wasn't too complex, but it had a nice four-measure countermelody that Harold Johnston had conceived. It was a simple place to begin a task that was much more involved than I would have first imagined. I remember Ovid reminding me that day of the "overtone series" and how it related to the orchestra. (So, there *was* a purpose for this scientific sidebar that had gone pretty much unnoticed by me in Theory 101!) I also remember from this first session that after having spent a generous amount of his time and hastily needing to bring things to a close, he pointed out the fact that I had a "false relation" in a voice part! Quickly his able fingers played a correction on his grand piano. Hopefully he did not notice my blushing red face! Serious music students all know that such a mistake is a "no, no!" in first year harmony. *Hmm*, I am sure he may have had second thoughts as to what he had gotten himself into after his spontaneous and kind offer of tutoring!

Regardless, several months later I again found myself knocking at his door. As always, this gracious and positive musician would welcome me with a broad smile, and we would sit at the kitchen table with my manuscripts before us. Since we were doing orchestrations, I would record from my computer the orchestral sounds produced by an early "Proteus 2" sound module—which at that time in the early nineties seemed to me, as a novice, to be fairly "cutting-edge." Of course, Ovid had all the sounds of the "real deal" embedded in his ear, so my recordings were no doubt slightly annoying with their unrealistic and inconsistent levels. Amazingly, he rarely complained, and over time my engineering skills eventually improved in trying to "conquer technology," as sound engineer friend Johnny Marshall used to jest. Johnny is another genius to whom I owe much for his patience and willingness to explain what he was doing as he worked his own magic on the recording that actually came to fruition a few years later.

My second piece for lesson number two with Ovid was one of the last that I had completed in California. It was a vocal duet for tenor and baritone on the hymn "How Great Thou Art." As we sat listening and following the score, I remember as if it were yesterday that Ovid suddenly stood up, smiled, and said, "*Now,* we have something to talk about!" I would like to think he saw a glimmer of promise in that moment! It was such a privilege and honor to continue year after year with this private instruction from the best of the best! He never would change his initial fee of fifty dollars for two to three hours of tutoring, despite my offering more. I am thankful that God blessed me with this gift because it encourages my heart and soul that He really *is* guiding the steps of my life, even when I am unaware.

Lest one grow too weary and wonder how this all fits in with the two chairs and *Tapestry,* of all things, I will jump forward a couple of years, not long after the recording entitled *Stormy Winds,* sung by Robert McFarland and Michael Sylvester. As with any serious study, one must have an incentive to keep working, learning, and growing. I initially considered tackling a work highlighting the stories of three or four hymn writers in a musical setting inspired by what I had seen presented at the International Nazarene Convention held in California in the late 1980s. Created and performed by well-known musicians D. Paul Thomas and his wife Janet, their work was a brilliant and moving biography of Fanny Crosby. Also featured in this musical were the talents of a small chorus. Two of the members of this chorus were old friends, Steve and Debbie Burwell, whom I recognized from my days at Azusa Pacific College. At this same gathering, Harold Johnston and I had the thrill of hearing our arrangement of "Jesus Shall Reign" played by Carolyn Steele, organist, and Evonne Neuenschwander, pianist. It was a "first" for me to hear someone else perform music I had arranged.

We continued to enjoy our serene surroundings in Texas. As it would happen, I took a bad fall when accidentally tripping over some pillows on the family room floor. A few months later I found myself undergoing back surgery as the result of a late-detected staphylococcus infection from a diagnostic discogram at the local hospital. Forced to lay low that next summer, I had lots of spare time to read and continue mulling over project ideas to pursue in continuing my studies with Ovid.

In the process of researching a number of hymn writers, I happened to read a bit about Martin Luther. I discovered that our small church library had a lengthy and well-known book on him. As I began to read more in depth, I was fascinated with his colorful story, and the idea to focus on a work just about him took shape. I also began to wonder why, growing up in an evangelical church, I never recall hearing more than a brief reference to the *Ninety-five Theses*. As I continued to read, I began to jot down notes and lyric ideas that were inspired by his many documented words and experiences.

One sticky problem which early on seemed impossible to surmount was: How do you write a musical that only has one woman as a main character and only much, much later in the story? For that reason I was tempted to give up on this idea completely. One day, however, my eyes fell upon an obscure and almost unnoticed reference to Luther's rather unromantically conceived marriage to the former nun Catherine and how strangely and unexpectedly it eventually prospered into a very loving union. She even worked his portrait into a "tapestry!"

Her tapestry was the spark that impressed on my mind a means of bringing to life such a historical character with his "feet of clay," as Ovid would later say! Catherine, as well as Philip, Luther's later and longtime friend, could be found in the narrative from its beginning until they stepped onto the stage of history themselves. As Catherine put the finishing touches on her tapestry, she and Philip remembered together, providing consolation to each other that evening of the day they had laid their beloved Martin to rest "beneath the pulpit that he loved so much."

I soon began a serious attempt to wade deeply through more sixteenth-century history toward the goal of finding a musical means of sequencing the events into a story. My sister Julie came to visit a few weeks later that summer as I was struggling to put phrases together to create the beginning *Tapestry* theme. It was her wonderful way with words that created the "fine-twined linen" result of Catherine's "at first uneven and coarse" stitches on the portrait of her husband Martin Luther as she would "sit beside him by the fireside in the evenings."

When fall arrived, I was once again scheduling composition lessons every few months. Ovid was in continual demand as a concert artist, flying somewhere most weekends to perform. Somehow he was always willing to carve out some extra hours every few months. Over the years our family came to love Ovid and Laura very much. At least once a year I would have them over for dinner. Admittedly, culinary arts have never been my passion, but I *did* always enjoy coming up with special dishes to try out on them. They were always so appreciative.

On one of those dinner occasions, I asked Ovid if I could borrow the duo piano arrangement of "The Music of the Night" from *The Phantom of the Opera* to use for a community program. He said he did not have a printout due to the fact that copyright issues would prevent its publication without fees. He and Stephen just played their memorized, improvised setting they had devised together. However, he asked me to go sit at my piano. He pulled up a chair nearby and proceeded to talk me through the ideas, and then I was to take it from there and develop my own rendition. I did, and it ended up being one of my most enjoyed settings. How gracious, accommodating, and kind of this extraordinary artist to be so willing to share his "trade secrets" with another just to help them succeed in every way.

Two or three times a year, Laura and I would meet for one of our "famous lunches," which more often than not found us chatting and laughing about almost anything that had to do with the then current state of the "worship arts," even if we could change nothing!

The first morning I arrived with my briefcase laden with those initial *Tapestry* attempts, I was a little unsure of what Ovid might feel about my new project and was somewhat hesitant about showing it to him. We went through the beginning two or three pieces on the table before him while listening to my cassette demo without too much discussion. Then nodding, he calmly said, "You know, I think you may have something here with this idea. Of course, you must definitely include a rousing rendition of 'Ein Feste Burg'!"

SLOWLY, BUT SURELY, I continued along year by year with the gradual creation of *Tapestry*. Not too far into this project a friend and neighbor, Mary Fargo, a former Catholic herself, offered to ask a local priest, Dr. John Sommerfield, for information as to what he might know of the typical ordination ceremony of a sixteenth-century monk. Father Sommerfield was an acquaintance of hers who taught at the University of Dallas. It was remarkable to me that he would take it upon himself to travel to another state to research in great detail and photocopy from old church archives an actual ordination service! I wrote to thank him profusely but never had a response or chance to meet him personally. It has also been enlightening to me that some Catholic brethren and friends readily admit they do not regard Martin Luther as a heretic for shedding light—at least on the corruption and abuses rampant in the Roman Church at that time in history.

OUR FRIENDS AND FAMILY often joke about the numerous homes we have lived in throughout the years. I am afraid there is a story to tell about every one of those homes—and a valid reason for moving on.

Our favorite Texas residence was the stately Georgian colonial home sitting on the top of a hill in the community called River Oaks in Fairview. The beautiful natural trees on the one-acre lot were abundant. It had been vacated for almost two years by the famed wrestler Dusty Rhodes and taken over by the bank. It was hard for me to imagine a wrestler having lived in such a classic traditional home. It needed lots of "elbow grease" and yard work, but the price was like a dream for Californians who were used to exorbitant prices and a flat piece of wood as baseboard trim! It is without saying that the abundant and lovely crown moldings and woodwork throughout blew us away!

One day, we impulsively decided to stop when we saw a man coming out the door of the vacant house. He was just a realtor there for some other reason, but he agreed to let us in. We were sure this home could not be in our price range. Of course, we immediately loved it! It had all the additional spaces so hard to find for a family of five that must make room for themselves as well as for pianos, organs, computers, etc. It was a "cliff-hanger" for a few months. Not too long after we had made our offer, others wanting the home seemed to appear out of nowhere and were willing to pay more!

At the last possible minute, our home down the road sold and the bank agreed to let us have the house for the price we had agreed upon initially—which was rather unusual to say the least. This was the one home in our long crazy history of real estate "ventures" that held no unhappy surprises or fixes. The rest is all massive material for another "book!"

Five to six years later, I was teaching a piano student from the town of Westin, about thirty minutes away. At a student recital, the girl's father remarked as he was leaving, "I am the carpenter who did the woodworking on this very house when it was built!"

IT WAS QUITE BY SURPRISE that Bill learned of another piano sitting in an empty duplex in Richardson, Texas. I don't remember who had mentioned this to him or why, but we decided to check it out, since a second piano would be helpful in my teaching studio. The Kawai was still being used by our church and would someday go to Melody, who was now enrolled as an elementary education major with a minor in music at Mid-America Christian University in Oklahoma City. The large expansive living room had plenty of space to accommodate another instrument. Our knowledgeable piano technician who had restored the bargain Steinway to tip-top shape, Joe Tom McDonald, offered to meet us the next afternoon to check it out. The owner wanted to remove the old piano so that he could free the space for boarders.

When I first laid eyes on the dusty old grand sitting there, my heart sank. Just pressing a few keys set off the shrill "boing" of strings popping and breaking. We were stunned and not sure what to say to the owner standing there with us. With quiet shrewdness, Joe Tom asked us to step outside a minute to discuss this matter. When we stood a few moments on the porch outside he said, "Calmly offer him less than the four thousand dollars to take it off his hands. This is an old Chickering from the 1920s! It will be a magnificent instrument when I restring and regulate it." We took his word for it, and the man was thrilled to have it go for three thousand dollars! So for another two thousand dollars to have Joe Tom restore it, we had a second seven-foot piano worth thousands more! I had no idea at the time how useful and enjoyed this piano would be in the coming years! Truly, another one of God's underserved and unexpected blessings!

ONE DAY AT A LESSON, Ovid handed me a flyer advertising "A Musical Tour of Europe" to be hosted by none other than Nielson and Young! He invited Bill and me to consider traveling with this small tour group to visit famous musical landmarks on the "trip of a lifetime" while listening to concerts by Nielson and Young! My husband and I mulled it over for a while and debated whether we could manage it. It was a little more money than any vacation we had ever taken but certainly reasonable.

Not too long after, I was struck with a sudden idea. Would this tour travel anywhere near Wittenberg? What better way to visualize a stage production! Of course, I doubted whether we could just take off from the tour and go it alone—but it was worth asking about! When I approached Ovid with that possibility, he thought it just might be doable on a day when it would not be too far to consider renting a car, traveling on the autobahn, and spending a day "doing our thing." That sold us! We signed up for the trip and even convinced my sister Julie and brother-in-law Bob to come to Dallas and go with us! While I was thinking out of the box (my usual way, more often than not), I also knew that the Czech Republic was near Vienna, and why not try to meet my grandmother's relatives on my dad's side? As it turned out, we had one more free day and permission for another side adventure that really made this the triple trip of a lifetime!

Our dad's cousin, Jan Drimal, DrSc., was a Slovak scientist and physician/pharmacologist specializing in cardiovascular research. We traveled by train from Vienna, Austria, to Bratislava, Slovakia, where he greeted us at the train station and gave us a mini tour of the sights in Bratislava. Our final stop was in front of the famous St. Martin's Cathedral where significant events had been celebrated, such as the crowning of Hungarian kings. When we tried to gain entry to the cathedral, filmmakers were making the movie called *The Peacemaker*. Jan tried to convince them that we were "important" (?!) people from the United States and that we had come all these miles to see this historical place. Not surprisingly, they were unconvinced, and we were unable to go inside.

Eventually we pulled up in front of a stark-looking, gray high-rise building of multiple stories and all squeezed into one of the tiniest elevators on which I had ever ridden. The elevator stopped, and we were soon standing outside the door of our relatives' apartment.

Jan spoke English, but his wife Vera did not, yet her smiles and warmth lessened the linguistic challenges. Their youngest son, a teenager at the time, still lived with them. I remember that the walls of this small living/dining room were lined from floor to ceiling with books. There was one small bathroom and kitchen. This was not what one would usually think of as being "a doctor's home" by western standards. Julie and I slept that night in their master bedroom, so I do not know where they would have slept themselves—

if they did at all! They were so gracious to us. Once known as Czechoslovakia, Slovakia and the Czech Republic were now two separate countries. The effects of socialism were disturbing to me. Jan told us that he had to chain his car to a post every night or it would be gone the next day! How blessed we are to live in a free America!

As we were leaving the next morning, I handed Jan a cassette tape of *Stormy Winds* in appreciation of their hospitality. A year later, after sending them a Christmas greeting, I was surprised when he responded to my letter and mentioned that his son, Daniel, had enjoyed the recording so much that he played the music over and over again. I was moved in my heart to witness again the universal power of music bridging any language barrier.

The next destination on our trip was Wittenberg, Germany. I will never forget the excitement that welled up inside me as we first stepped inside the ancient but still regal Castle Church. We found ourselves standing beneath the ornate and massive raised pulpit that Luther loved so much. A large rectangular concrete burial marker denoted the resting place of the great reformer lying permanently beneath the church floor. We spent some time just walking around the interior, taking in the statues of the colleagues who were in solidarity with Martin Luther while trying to imagine what it would have been like to live during those tumultuous years of upheaval and drastic change. After some time had passed, we strolled outside and along the same street toward the monastery and the university on the opposite end of the town. This afforded us the opportunity to view and experience Wittenberg as it would pretty much have been almost five hundred years earlier. We passed by the home of Luther's beloved friend and fellow scholar, Philip Melancthon, and it all seemed a bit surreal to me. Who would have thought that Marilyn Lee Singer Thompson would ever arrive on the other side of the world because of a matching chair?

A FEW WEEKS PRIOR to the European adventure, I was standing in line at a department store at the Collin Creek Mall about thirty minutes south of Fairview, Texas, waiting to purchase a large handbag for the trip. The clerk, needing change for the cash register, stepped away for five to ten minutes leaving a tall, pleasant young woman in line behind me. We began to chat a bit. Being six feet in height, I was interested in what she was telling me as to where she had successfully found a pair of hard-to-find proportioned, longer-length slacks. That was the extent of our conversation when the clerk returned to her cash register.

About six months following the European trip, Bill and I had taken his visiting cousin to explore the unique little shops in old downtown McKinney. Upon entering an interesting shop of old lamps, I was surprised to suddenly see that same tall and friendly lady who had visited with me at the department store before our departure to Europe. We laughed at seeing each other again so far from the first meeting. Spontaneously I said, "Wow, this must be an omen of something meant to be. We should exchange telephone numbers." I wrote down my phone number, and she in turn handed me a business card that revealed her to be a realtor. I did not look at it real closely, so I did not notice her address. Upon arriving back home, I put it in my desk drawer, where it sat for another six months.

In the meantime, a member of Grace church gave my phone number to their neighbor, Dorothy Lankenau, as she was looking for someone with whom to study improvisation. Dorothy was an experienced organist who had played in Chicago before coming to Texas, where she and her husband could be near their children. We developed an immediate bond because we both found ourselves a bit displaced, being that neither of us had found a musical niche in the area.

She was attending the Custer Road United Methodist Church when we first became acquainted. One Good Friday she gave my name to the church organist, Kay Sendrey, when there was the need for a pianist to fill in as the "harp" for their choral presentation of the Dubois *Seven Last Words of Christ*. I subsequently saw Kay on several occasions connected with musical events. She lived in the nearby large suburb of Plano.

I had worked as a team with Dorothy in a couple of short interim positions, one being at Spring Valley United Methodist Church in Dallas. She had asked me to share the duties with her early on in our friendship. During that brief period of time, I met a vibrant soprano in the choir named Lynne Swafford, who offered to add her voice to the recording I had started that would eventually serve as a *Tapestry* demo. She made the forty-five-minute trip to Fairview four to five times to assist me. Dorothy was an unflagging supporter of my musical compositions and a treasured blessing in my life. We enjoyed a lasting friendship until her death from cancer in June 2011. I still miss her!

One day my eyes fell on the business card from Pam Reaves, the realtor I had met on two occasions. I was prompted from within to give her a call, and we decided we would visit the McKinney Square and eat at the Pantry restaurant—a landmark of the still small Texas town. She offered to stop by our home and drive us to our destination. When I greeted her at the door, her eyes lit up as she stepped inside and noticed the two grand pianos facing each other in the living room. She told me that she had been a composition major at Hardin-Simmons University, having come from California a number of years ago! We couldn't believe we shared so much in common.

As we chatted away in the car, she told me that she also lived in Fairview. After a few minutes of conversation, she related that she and a friend sang in the Rich-Tone Chorus, a professional women's ensemble in nearby Richardson. The friend's mother, Dorothy Lankenau, was an organist who had moved to Fairview a few years back and wished she could find a regular position! Needless to say, all of this coincidence was quite amazing. The lovely harp that sits today in our living room is all because of her. (Pam insists that I, like she, could become a harpist?!)

ꞰROM TIME TO TIME the words of Corrie Ten Boom came to mind: "When God closes a door, he always opens a window!" For the next ten years it seemed that my "window" was to be the unexpected opportunity of writing over a dozen keyboard books for major sacred publishing houses and to continue doing so even today. Why me? I do not know because I am not, as I have stated before, a prodigy of obvious extraordinary abilities. However, God put others in my path that shared their remarkable gifts with someone who loved music—especially the message and beauty that it brought to Christian worship. There is no way I can ever repay those who have taught and mentored, especially when hard-pressed themselves to find many idle moments! I am sure they have probably shaken their heads and stifled a few moments of laughter.

One example stands out to me when early on I was learning about timpani and all the colorful percussion touches that enhance the orchestra. I was attempting to come up with a "killer timpani" to add variety. I recall that after patiently enduring the entire piece, Dr. Young said, "Well," in his always kind and positive manner, "I did like a lot of things I was hearing, but I have to admit that our timpanist seemed to enter from out of nowhere to go into an abrupt and complete frenzy for his big moment!" or words to that effect. I find myself chuckling even today and wondering how this accomplished composer could even halfway choke down a huge guffaw of laughter that would surely have been a struggle to contain after enduring my amateur treatment of this stately member of the percussion! The only redeeming quality may have been that it was at least passionate! Hopefully there were more times when some of my "grand ideas" revealed that I was paying attention to my teacher.

When I finally had my first rough draft of *Tapestry* completed and recorded, Ovid suggested that he take it to Robert Rucker at Park Cities Presbyterian Church in Dallas. Robert was at that time the minister of music and was also well known for his church and stage productions. He responded with an enthusiastic and positive "thank you" while admitting that mounting a large production like this was too much for the church at that time. We were both disappointed, but I know now that it was not meant to be at that juncture because of all which has followed since that first inquiry.

On one occasion at a lesson, Ovid handed me a book entitled *By Faith Alone*, a lovely hardbound devotional compiled from sermons, commentaries, and other devotional writings of Martin Luther. This thoughtful gift was from a pianist/composer named Robin Thomas from West Monroe, Louisiana. Robin had been coming for a year or so to periodically study piano with Stephen Nielson and now was also studying with Ovid as well. He thought that we should meet, and it was not long afterward that we met at a performance given at Aldersgate United Methodist

Church in Carrollton, Texas. I liked her immediately. Soon she would also include a visit to our home when she made the four-hour drive to the area. We enjoyed practicing with one another and seemed to feel music together with relative ease. During the next six to seven years, several opportunities arose to play church concerts together.

Robin was very active in the music of Louisiana and invited me to participate with her at a local music teachers' association meeting to play several Rachmaninoff duets along with some other Russian composers. She also invited me that same weekend to perform with her in the annual "Keyboard Kaleidoscope" concert that the large First Baptist Church of West Monroe hosted every year. Therefore, the next year was spent creating orchestral manuscripts for their large church orchestra.

As further preparation for these two concerts, she invited me to travel with her to Dallas for a number of joint lessons with the incredible Stephen Nielson. Up until that time, I had only a casual introduction to this world-class performer *and* teacher—a combination that is not always found in one person. Like his recently departed mother Lois, herself vital and active for over ninety years, his teaching excellence is imparted with enthusiasm and passion.

I still can recall the trembling hands and "pretzel fingers" I experienced on my first private lesson with Stephen. I am not sure he had ever seen someone quite as nervous as I was that day. Miraculously, I guess he must have seen some evidence of technique lurking somewhere in the background in order to allow me to continue as a student! Also, since there was considerable distance between our homes, I deeply appreciated his willingness to allow me come to his studio on the not-too-frequent occasions when I was able to make the journey.

It was customary for Stephen's students to have formal recitals several times a year. One in particular stands out in my mind. Robin and I were to play a duo piano setting of "The Dance of the Petits Garcons" from the *Polovtsian Dances* by Alexander Borodin. As we pulled up to Stephen's home that afternoon, Robin commented on a familiar car and exclaimed, "That looks like *Ovid's* car!" I did not pay too much attention because I thought it was just an unlikely coincidence. However, as we opened the door to enter we spotted a smiling Ovid waving from a back corner of the living room. Wow, was that ever pressure! Soon after I learned that in all the years of Stephen's student recitals, his colleague had never before been in attendance—until that day!

WHILE LIVING IN FAIRVIEW, TEXAS, those ten years, I enjoyed being the accompanist for Robert McFarland in his occasional sacred concerts. He would sing some of his famous opera villain solos intermixed with selections from the hymn arrangements that were created for him a few years earlier. Each performance has special memories of the unexpected—which I have now come to expect! The one that still remains at the top of the list was a formal concert for paid subscribers in Tyler, Texas, for the Marvin United Methodist Church.

The evening before, as we were sitting with several others eating our dinner, I suddenly realized that I had left my black concert apparel hanging near our home's back door (so I would not forget it) at least four hours away. Well, forget it I did, and now I had nothing to wear the following Sunday night except the casual outfit I was wearing at the moment. It was 8:30 p.m. and the nearby Dillard's Department Store closed at 9:00 p.m.! Somehow, in fifteen minutes with Robert's help, I was able to find a lovely long black skirt and matching sequined top that actually fit and was far nicer than any outfit I had ever owned! (No small feat, especially when you are six feet tall!)

ANOTHER HOME HAVING AN INTERESTING TALE to tell was the patio home. This was to be the move-in-ready, small, no stress, last home—and the only *new* home we ever purchased! Bill decided that it was time to scale down since the children were now in college and he would soon retire. Robin was still coming to town during the time we made this move. Amid the over 150 visits from the home builder to fix the major problems that were almost a daily occurrence, a nice couple moved into the new home built next door to ours. Soon after meeting our lovely neighbors, Keith and Loydelle Hopkins, I learned that she was the same esteemed conductor, Dr. Loydelle Hopkins, from West Monroe, Louisiana. Robin knew her and praised her fine reputation. Now what is the likelihood of such a coincidence! The homebuilder was reputable and stood behind his product, so it became a beautiful home for the *next* person to buy. The charm for us had worn off. We also found that the increasing noise of the road behind our back fence was not peaceful or tranquil anymore. It was *never* supposed to become a main drag!

During the three years of living in our aforementioned patio home, we received a newsletter from Stonebriar Church in Frisco, Texas. We had visited there one Sunday and were put on the mailing list for a short time. When I opened the newsletter, I saw a familiar lady on the third page. I couldn't believe it, but it just had to be Debbie Burwell from Azusa days—the same Debbie Burwell who had been in the Fanny Crosby Story sixteen years ago in California along with her husband Steve. As I found out by further inquiry, they were now in Texas, only ten miles or so west of our home. She had been hired as the Children's Director for Stonebriar Church—Chuck Swindoll's current place of pastoral ministry! We, of course, renewed our friendship, and Steve agreed to be the voice of Luther's close friend Philip Melancthon on my *Tapestry* demo that was always a continuing "work in progress." Steve continued to do an excellent job leading one of the choirs at the mega church in Frisco.

After hunting on and off for almost a year, we found a "fixer upper" a few miles east from our patio home and got the old elbow grease moving again! The home had been vacant for several years. It was a little oddball in some respects, but the space inside could accommodate the two grand pianos and organ that always complicated our searches for suitable homes. We thought the location, which for years had remained a more remote and less densely populated section of town, would surely continue to remain so. A nearby pond visible from our back living room window and the easily accessible tree-shaded walking trails clinched the deal.

Two years later, we returned home from a visit to Oklahoma to see Melody and family and discovered a message on our answering machine: "Marilyn, this is Kay Sendrey. I am calling from…" She named our old address!

"We love it here!" (Apparently our patio home had now been sold again. This time to Kay Sendrey and her husband, and of course she was crazy about the musical wallpaper in the powder bath that we had chosen when the home was first built.) Kay, until recent years, was still the organist at Custer Road United Methodist Church and played the magnificent pipe organ, named in her honor.

Around the same time that I received the above message from Kay, a huge wall rising thirty to forty feet tall appeared along the east boundary of our housing community in an attempt to hide the rows of shops and restaurants which began to appear with increasing rapidity. This resulted in longer waits in attempting to exit from our development to access the main roads for travel. The final straw occurred a year later when taking a walk toward the pond one morning. I happened to cast a glance across the water to enjoy the view of the many tall trees for which this area was known, only to find them absent and replaced instead by the sight of numerous cars speeding along the main southbound 75 expressway toward Dallas! A few weeks later, an enormous multistoried building began to be erected. Wow, the city had come to the sleepy suburb in the blink of an eye!

Disheartened, we took a drive not too long afterward and, thanks to a tip from a country property realtor who pointed us northwest, we discovered Lake Kiowa. Once again we had to decide if we could endure the headaches of one more move. The fact that we would be so central now to all of our children caused us to dive in feet first and take one more chance on another bank repo. After all, we had to maintain our current "gypsy" reputation that our friends and family had started to attach to our name! Even with the dandelions and weeds, which were five-feet tall in many instances (no exaggeration!), we signed on the dotted line. The home that we were vacating took only a few weeks to sell and not the usual year to find just the right buyer. (The home was dubbed a "loft house" by one young couple who eagerly competed for the sale against an out-of-state client. Well, I admitted to the fact that it was a different kind of house! Honestly, we never intended to become "land barons" wheeling and dealing with all manner of homes and locations, but our lives seem to travel and be destined for the unexpected at a moment's notice!)

ᏴEFORE MOVING IN 2008 to Lake Kiowa in the Gainesville area, we enjoyed almost five years with the nurturing congregation of Trinity Presbyterian Church in McKinney. I was employed at that time as pianist/organist. The job came quite suddenly. A year or so before, I had sent out a few letters to nearby churches to submit my name as a substitute pianist/organist. I remember feeling a bit at loose ends with no real opportunities to share much in music. I never had any response until a year later, when I received an invitation to visit with Heather Harrity, the music director at Trinity Presbyterian, just down the road a mile or two from us. The church was in need of an organist/pianist.

The very next day I hobbled in to see Heather. (I say "hobbled" because I had broken my right little toe and was walking in the wooden shoe I needed to wear until the break was healed.) Heather was a very passionate musician and the daughter of two concert artists. She had a very extensive musical background, along with a devoutly committed heart to the Lord. We chatted a bit, and then she had me sight read a choral anthem and finally play a sacred solo. I chose my arrangement of "My Tribute." True to my usual form in new situations, I was a bit nervous. My hands trembled somewhat, but she must have overlooked it, as she almost immediately told me I was hired, providing the board approve her choice after my first trial Sunday. On my way out the door she said, "By the way, you *do* play the organ?" "Yes," I replied with as much confidence as I could muster—while in my mind recalling that it had been at least fifteen years since I had touched an organ and all the while thinking, *lucky for me I can't audition today with a wooden shoe!*

My trial Sunday was delayed a few weeks until my toe healed, so you know what I did, I am sure—practice, practice, and more practice! I didn't pull out all the stops on that first Sunday, but they seemed satisfied and hired me anyway. I gleaned much experience over the next few years, and it felt so good to be working again in music ministry at a local church!

Heather once joked to me about her "high-strung Hungarian temperament." Admittedly, she at times could be a bit of a "taskmaster"—especially when a musical deadline was approaching. I received a taste of that characteristic not too long after I was into my job. It was during the first Christmas, when she ambitiously decided on presenting a portion of Handel's *Messiah* with our twenty or so mostly inexperienced choral singers. She was truly amazing in her perseverance to make this happen, and the choir did learn their advanced level parts quite well. She had scheduled the dress rehearsal on Saturday morning preceding the Sunday service the following day.

As Bill and I were going out the door that morning to make the five-minute drive, the phone rang. Bill spontaneously decided that he should answer. Unfortunately, it was a call that needed his attention for five or six minutes.

As a result, we were seven minutes tardy to rehearsal. I was not overly concerned at first, since I figured that it always takes a few minutes for any group to assemble and organize in a new space outside the usual rehearsal room. However, when we walked into the sanctuary, they were all in place and actually rehearsing with Heather at the piano.

Honestly, I had never been late before and was not prepared for how upset she became that morning. As I hurried down the aisle to the piano, she did not ask if we had any emergency or valid reason for being late. Instead she glared rather fiercely, abruptly got up from the piano, and marched to take her position at the director's stand. I must laugh now, but at the time I could barely read the mass of notes on the page, and my hands shook because her tempo was lightning speed! That "Hungarian" temperament was being felt! Any pianist who has played this revered work knows the speed limits realistically possible when attempting to read all vocal lines concurrently from an open score. This was particularly true while rehearsing the florid lines of "For Unto Us a Child is Given." I expected to be fired on the spot, barely having been there a few months!

Of course, I realize fully that my memory might be *slightly* exaggerating those moments! All kidding aside, Heather was such a God-driven person in countless ways. I still grieve her early death from ovarian cancer at age thirty-eight. Her bravery and unwavering faith through so much suffering was truly an inspiring testament, and she will always be remembered by so many.

When Tami Holland eventually became the new music director, she was generous about affording me several opportunities to branch out from my accompanist duties to put together both a production of *Amahl and the Night Visitors* and an orchestral-duo piano concert. She also encouraged my efforts with a string ensemble that I enjoyed organizing. Her beautiful voice reflected her equally beautiful spirit.

When I recall my few years with Trinity, I think of precious saints like Dr. Jim and Marian Wilson and his well-prepared and enlightening Sunday school class, prayer warrior Jessie Rodrigues, the embracing Ray and Francis Wood, now retired senior pastor Patrick McCoy, pastor emeritus Don Andrews and his late wife Frieda, the late Bill and Ann Dowdy and the "The Sinner's Pew" small group meetings held quite often in their historical childhood home. And I cannot omit mentioning the irrepressible and always smiling redhead Barbara Lindsay, with whom I shared many walks, talks, and a treasured friendship. Trinity will always remain my church family in so many ways.

Lake Kiowa is a serene and idyllic country setting. We appreciate this more central location to our children and the new little grandbabies blessing our lives. At the same month we were making our move to this area, the Youngs were moving back to their Illinois roots after many years in the Dallas area. So all good things come to an end whether we wish them to or not, and I needed to rejoice with our friends that there was a new chapter ahead for them as well as for us. At first I really missed my employment at Trinity. Finding myself with no weekly commitment, I began to revisit Luther a bit. I cannot help but be impressed with the wealth of fine musical talent abounding in the Gainesville area that rivals many cities near the Dallas Metroplex. I continue to learn and grow in new areas as the list of special new friends and kindred spirits grows.

A couple of years after coming to this area, I felt the desire to start a community orchestra that could involve known and/or unused talent in the community. My vision was to gather and train a pool of musicians who would be available for civic and church programs. I was hoping that such a group might inspire adults of all ages to either dig out their old instruments and play again or be the incentive for current high school age and older students to keep growing and gaining proficiency.

The only way I could round up enough players to commit to a first concert was to create practice MP3 recordings for everyone to use on their own time. They all finally agreed to one rehearsal and a concert to follow that same day. To fill out the orchestra a bit more, I put out a call to friends and acquaintances I have known and worked with through the years. They, like myself, love any opportunity to make music together. Along with three well-known and loved pianists known to this community (Carolyn Hook, Peggy O'Neill, and Glen Wilson), I also invited participation of local church choirs to sing three or four choral arrangements with the orchestra. Barbara Brady and her amazing choir from First Presbyterian Church came in full force. Combined with our own Westminster Presbyterian Church choir and a few from several other congregations, the choir loft was overflowing. Charles Hart, with his beautiful tenor voice, was also there to assist as a soloist and choir singer. When the orchestra came to rehearsal that afternoon, I wasted at least half an hour moving stands and chairs to make room for all of them. Actually, I had no idea that we would have such a great number of participants. There were actually more on the platform than in the audience that night, but it did not seem to matter to anyone.

I had written to Ovid asking him to give me advice on how to direct an orchestra, since my orchestras have for the most part been created mostly in my home studio. (He must have thought I was crazy to attempt such a feat under these circumstances.) Always positive and optimistic, however, he advised me that I should first get myself a baton! "Since you are the one who has written and knows the music, you are the best one to direct it!" were his words. Of course I took his advice. He assured me that my "ace in the hole" was my three keyboard players who would help me carry it off—no matter what discord or confusion might happen in the orchestra pit.

An added support, John Dill, current organist at Stonebriar Church, native of Gainesville and installer of every pipe organ in town, appeared to assist on the Wicks organ. (His mother-in-law Trisha, then a member of our church choir, had no doubt done a little "friendly persuasion" to talk him into making an appearance.) Thus, we had four strong keyboard players that day!) Also, Kent Hillman, absolutely one of the most skilled percussionists I have heard, was there to add his "bells and whistles" and play timpani, on loan by wind instrumental professor Marty Kobucks from the local college. It was an effort of so many generous people whom I did not really know too well at this point.

I began to wave my baton with fear and trepidation. Would it even resemble music? I was overcome with relief and total amazement when I heard the large diverse group of players begin the strains of "Chariots of Fire." It really was a lovely sound! We had time for only one run-through of every piece. The choir sang their hearts out, and it was a memorable time. It was pretty incredible for the lunacy of basically no rehearsal! What a happy surprise to turn around at the end of this concert and find my three favorite friends, the Wilsons, the Dowdys, and the Lindsays, making their way toward me, having traveled the hour-plus drive that evening from McKinney to support and encourage our efforts.

*T*HREE YEARS LATER, the Youngs returned for an unexpected visit on the occasion of our youngest daughter Melissa's wedding. She was marrying Darin Bjork, who actually had grown up in Orange County, California, and moved to Fairview, Texas, about the same time we did those many years ago. Their lives paralleled each other through school, even so far as to ride the same school bus. The wedding was going to take place in Darin's family church in (would you believe it?) Custer Road United Methodist Church, where Kay Sendrey was organist!

After Melissa had chosen the music, Stephen Nielson graciously agreed to be the pianist. When I brought the music to Stephen a couple of weeks before the wedding date, I told him that it would have been wonderful if Ovid still lived in Texas and could be the organist with him on the Wicks pipe organ. I felt that I could not impose on him to travel all this way back from Illinois. Suddenly Stephen's eyes lit up. Stepping to his nearby desk, he picked up and opened his personal calendar, which was always meticulously up-to-date. Smiling, he said, "Ovid is coming that very weekend to play for a small graduation ceremony at Laura's old Christian school where she taught while living in Texas. I have a feeling if you contact him right away, you may find this is God at work!"

I hurried home and raced to the computer to dash off an email. In less than fifteen minutes I had his enthusiastic *"Yes!"* Of course, Kay graciously agreed that Ovid should be the organist. What an unforgettable day! Melissa was thrilled to experience her long-anticipated bridal recessional to the jubilant strains of the "Widor Organ Toccata" (and much more!), not to mention the combined talents and music of Nielson and Young! Naturally, our friend Robert McFarland was there to add his masterful baritone solos. Not by choice did the "Singer Sisters trio" want to be in this group of elite musicians that day, but Melissa insisted that she wanted her aunts and mother to resurrect "The Lord is My Shepherd"—the trio she remembered from her childhood. It was pretty hard to have any kind of breath support for singing that day, and I definitely breathed a sigh of relief when our musical moment was over!

Now I could sit back and relax as the mother of the bride to just listen and appreciate the lovely rendering of my choral setting of the old poem "How Do I Love Thee" By Elizabeth Barrett Browning. The music was composed at Melissa's request to be sung by our extended family that had traveled the lengthy distance from California to share their music. My youngest sister Melinda was struggling physically at that time, but her gorgeous soprano voice soared above all that morning. It was the crowning touch of strength and beauty serving to blend the unaccompanied ensemble into the glorious sounds that echoed throughout the large church.

In October following Melissa's wedding, my sister Julie and I were able to take a spontaneous driving trip to

Illinois. Along with stops to see friends and relatives, we also enjoyed spending a fun couple of nights visiting with Ovid and Laura in their new home near Olivet University. Ovid was now the "artist in residence." We visited the campus and saw the recently installed pipe organ being readied for the upcoming dedicatory concert by him.

$\mathscr{S}$IX MONTHS LATER, I was in the final stages of planning another program for the following spring (and hoping for several rehearsals on this second attempt). Actually, I had prepared the music and MP3 recordings and had my finger on the "send" button to e-mail scores and ask for participation. At that moment, the call came regarding the medical emergency hospitalization of our three-year-old grandson Justin. The common influenza virus caused encephalitis resulting in his death four days later on January 24, 2011.

One of my last sweet remembrances of this precious and sensitive child occurred on a visit to his home the previous summer. That morning, as we were sitting in the family room, I noticed a toy keyboard nearby and decided to have some fun with our grandson. He loved to sing and, like our son many years ago, delighted in the clever Disney tunes from *The Jungle Book*. (I have memories of our Mark as a boy of that same age sitting at his pint-sized table on which his childhood phonograph rested. He was playing practically ad nauseam the recording of "The Bear Necessities.") As I began to play my recollection of the long-forgotten tune, Justin began to sing and prance to the lively music. Abruptly he stopped while shaking his head and laughing. I tried several times to coax him to begin again, only to have him continue to refuse. Suddenly he blurted out, "Grammie, that is just not *right!*"

By then, his mother had entered the room and said, "Mom, I think you may be leaving out a small line." After listening to her sing the omission, I laughed and said, "Oh yes, now I remember. Justin, you were exactly right on!" (So much for lifelong musician Grammie and her so-called skills. Justin would have no doubt put me to shame later on!) Now he could sing it as it should be sung—correctly; and so he did with all the exuberant joy of a three-year-old boy! His subsequent passing, coupled with two other extremely distressing family tragedies, caused me to put any plans for a second community orchestra concert on hold indefinitely. Perhaps there may eventually come a time when it might seem right to proceed again.

IN THE SUMMER OF 2011, our family had attended an outstanding performance of *The Sound of Music* under the direction of Shane Studdard, the local music professor at North Central Texas College in Gainesville—a real accomplishment for such a small community. Still feeling the sadness of losing little Justin the first of that year, our family had decided it might be uplifting to all to meet together and enjoy this beautiful and inspirational musical.

I felt compelled to send this professor an email to let him know how much it was appreciated by all of us. I had never personally spoken with him before except to briefly thank him for arranging the use of the NCTC First State Bank Performing Arts Center. The occasion was a duo-piano concert in which Carolyn Hook had invited me to participate several months before. She is a very experienced and skillful performer, originally from Oklahoma. I was honored to have enjoyed that performance opportunity and learned much from this collaboration. Mr. Studdard took care of all the promotional details with professional skill.

The following year I was surprised to receive an email from this same professor inviting me to be a guest accompanist for his newly-formed College Singers. He had organized this group from its inception with whoever showed up that first day of class—about nine students. I must admit

I was not feeling overly confident on that first day. It had been many years since I had been in an academic environment, and I was not sure what expectations this obviously perfectionistic director would hold. I had to laugh inside (or maybe cry, more likely). Almost from the moment I walked through the door, he had a recorder ready to roll in order, no doubt, to facilitate creating practice CD's for his class! *Gulp*!

The first October concert featured this little group singing a charming but uncomplicated assortment of folk tunes. It was a good place to begin with untrained and inexperienced young voices. However, this dynamic and gifted director soon began to work his own magic. As a result, the group began to grow, and their musicality increased phenomenally. By the following fall, they had become quite a fine-sounding ensemble. Their programs became more and more ambitious each year, even to the level of being chosen from auditioned school choirs across the nation on two separate occasions to perform at Walt Disney World in Orlando, Florida. They also participated in the Vivaldi *Gloria* performance at Carnegie Hall in New York City.

During this same time, another experience really stretched me out of my accompanist comfort zone again. I was filling in as interim choir director at the historic First United Methodist Church in Gainesville, Texas. Don Yeager, who was the pastor at that time, remembered my name from the letter I had previously sent to local churches recruiting volunteers for the aforementioned orchestra program months earlier. The church had found themselves suddenly in a bind for three months in 2013 without a choral director. If he had not been so nice and pleaded so hard, I might not have accepted. I had to resurrect my old college textbooks for that one, but the people were very supportive of my efforts.

While serving those few months, I became acquainted with Melodye McLeroy, one of two excellent accompanists employed by the church. To our mutual delight, we became close friends while discovering a common love of piano duos. We began to collaborate during that time and currently continue to do so frequently.

I WAS PLEASANTLY SURPRISED when an out-of-state Christian university committed to a performance of *Tapestry* in 2014. In anticipation, I devoted my spare time that summer to creating a rehearsal piano-vocal score. Of course, I was very excited about the prospect of a performance! Through the years our incredible baritone friend Robert McFarland had slowly put his voice on my *Tapestry* demos on the occasions he came through our town. He was a brilliant "Luther" who could sing anything! Historically Luther was a tenor, but I thought he needed to be a baritone in this instance to represent his "larger than life" character in the context of this musical/quasi opera into which things evolved.

Robert's enormous vocal range stretched my thinking and abilities beyond my usual skills. His input added the necessary vocal nuances, musical interpretation, and most importantly the spiritual understanding that hopefully would project to an audience and draw them in emotionally to identify with the inward struggles of this reluctant hero. As I still read his writings today, I am continually reminded that Luther, though far from perfect, is a man who should not be forgotten as the five hundred-year anniversary of the Protestant Reformation was to be upon us in 2017. In many respects, do we not seem to find ourselves in what may well be the most dangerous and turbulent time in the age-old battle of good vs. evil?

Early that next fall, I requested a meeting with Professor Studdard to get his professional advice on what I needed to do on my end to be organized and ready for a stage production. I was not sure what reaction he might have when I began playing for him a few short excerpts from my demo CD. However, his immediate response in hearing Robert's powerful baritone voice was, "Now, *that's* a singer!" I then asked him how best to begin the huge task of planning the staging directions. Many suggestions began flowing almost spontaneously as he drew upon his years of vast experience. When our meeting ended, I unexpectedly had another surprise, which I refer to as my second "Ovid Young moment." Professor Studdard graciously offered to meet with me weekly and listen to the complete work in its entirety so as to discuss specific details scene by scene. He refused to accept any monetary payment, although I would have willingly paid for this rare opportunity to benefit from another master. It is without saying that my life was continuing to be quite a "Tapestry Journey," as he began to call this venture.

At long last, I now come back to the nameless antique-appearing furniture item given to me many years prior. Shortly before the close of the current spring semester, I was working on one of my homework assignments from the professor—that being to organize, list, and gather pictures of all props for each scene. The first item which I had no idea how to describe was a sixteenth-century "bishop's faldstool," mentioned in the early priest ordination scene that Father John Sommerfield had copied for me many years prior. I turned to the trusty search engine Google, as one does quite automatically in our Internet age. Lo and behold, what appeared at the very top of the search results was an exact image of the mysterious ornate wooden folding stool that I had been carefully guarding all these years, handed to me by Ovid and Laura Young in exchange for the missing chair from their dining room set—several years before *Tapestry* was ever a conception!

For unknown and unexplained reasons, the performance did not happen at the university the spring of 2014 despite the promised premiere. I had no idea what was now ahead for *Tapestry*. However, Shane and I continued a few more weeks listening and discussing the work to the end. Just before I left his office that last evening, he pulled a couple of books from his shelf. While handing them to me, he said, "Whoever will be doing this, whether myself or someone else, will need a libretto such as these." "You mean that *you* would do it?!" I asked incredulously. "Yes!" he replied without hesitation. I can't do it this summer, but next summer would be possible, just on the eve of the five hundred-year anniversary of the Reformation.

And so we did, *and* of course Robert McFarland came to sing the role of "Luther" after all these many years! The "Ovid Young Chair," as I had come to affectionately call it, sat in a special position on the stage as well! I shall never forget the wonderful cast and chorus and their beautiful production under the consummate direction of Shane Studdard in the lovely First State Bank Center for the Performing Arts at North Central Texas College.

Regrettably, Dr. Young had too prematurely passed away in August 2014 (before knowledge of our eventual performances) following a valiant struggle with cancer. However, having learned of the "bishop's chair" before his death, he declared it a true miracle from God. Of course, this premiere was presented in his honor! It was an added joy to have Laura Young and their eldest son Kirk, Stephen and Carolyne Nielson, Don and Eleanor Whitsett, Steve and Debbie Burwell, and Robin Thomas in attendance, most of whom were personal colleagues of Ovid Young, along with our entire family and many cherished long-time friends.

I HAVE BEEN REMINDED quite often the past three years following this blessed occasion in my life how only God sees the future. We truly do not know what the next moment will bring. Three months after *Tapestry*, Bill suffered a stroke on December 28, 2017, that completely changed both of our lives. His memory and cognitive abilities were greatly affected. How grateful I am that he was well at the time of the performances!

The month preceding his affliction, we had decided that the smaller home we purchased two years prior with the intentions of enlarging was just not going to be possible financially. Although we loved it, there was just not enough space. We were "wall-to-wall everything!" (even after having sold or given away many items before leaving our prior home.) And for sure, a grand piano, a full-sized organ, and a large flat-screen TV could no longer cohabitate peacefully together in one living area! We made the decision to move to another home in Lake Kiowa.

There were a few repairs to be made to our current residence before listing it for sale, so it was up to me to take charge while Bill was in rehab for four months. I did not know where to begin (is putting it mildly!) My husband was the "engineer" of the family and was always on top of such tasks by nature. Now that was not possible and may never be again on Earth. But miracles *do* happen, as I can attest with certainty!

When I could delay no longer in finding a handyman, I opened the Kiowa Communique, our local newsletter, to a "sea" of ads. I was searching for someone to repair a stack of bricks that had been knocked over on a lamppost near our driveway entrance. My eyes fell on one that bore the title "Small Job Specialist." I said to myself, "*I'll just choose him!*" To his great credit, he promptly returned my phone call. Twenty minutes later, he was standing on our doorstep!

Little did I ever dream that this kind gentleman, Don Rogers, would turn out to be "Mr. Angel Man," as we have endearingly come to call him. We have no doubt that he was truly sent to us from God for some reason. It would take another entire book just to begin to relate the help and support this highly skilled, intelligent, and compassionate man has given us. He has assisted us in countless ways due to increasing difficulties brought about by Bill's dramatic health changes. We have now been over three years walking through quite unchartered territory.

I referred once to our "interesting" homes over the years and the many surprises lurking in the background. Life has certainly not ever been dull! The current residence probably tops them all, but thanks to Mr. Rogers, it has hope! Would you believe that our friend Don is also a fine musician! Amazingly, God even sent us an angel to fit both our personalities and passions!

I still marvel that such incomparable life-long encouragement and assistance has arisen from a rather eclectic collection of friends and fellow musicians. Why, even our longtime piano tuner, Joe Tom McDonald, was such a good sport and cheerfully, at a moment's notice (and in *one* perfect "take"!) added his colorful voice to my *Tapestry* demo "mix" one day just before stepping out the door to begin his long drive home.

Is there yet another unusual chapter waiting to be written in *My Tapestry Journey*? If so, there will be no doubt in my mind that it is Certainly *Not* an Accident!

$\mathcal{A}$S I REFLECT on the numerous and unlikely chance happenings of people and experiences that have been woven into my own life's story, I see them all contributing to this unique and surprising journey that God has seemingly ordained for me. (My sister Julie tells me that there are still way too many exclamation points, dashes, and quotation marks in this journal, but that is how I have seen my life. Undeniably, it has been full of surprises at every juncture!) What fun and rich memories are mine to treasure always, even if *Tapestry* had never received a public performance!

Many times I read from a devotional book taken from the teachings and sermons of Martin Luther, most of which still seem so contemporary and relevant today. Sooner or later, it seems that we are all brought to our knees and to the end of ourselves with the inevitable storms of life that can paralyze our emotions. We can be left shaking our fist at God and, like Martin Luther in his most despondent moments, demanding, "Why?"

In all honesty, I must admit that the past ten years, despite numerous blessings, have been among the most heart wrenching of my entire life. Honestly, there are many moments that I have yet to fully understand what God may be trying to teach me. I must remind myself that all of our individual personal tragedies seem to pale in comparison to the unthinkable sufferings that are daily occurrences in all parts of the world—splashed across our screens by television and social media.

Quite often in my childhood church, my sisters and I would sing as a trio:

When upon life's billows you are tempest-tossed,
When you are discouraged, thinking all is lost,
Count your many blessings, name them one by one,
And it will surprise you what the Lord hath done.

The above words no longer just "roll off my tongue" anymore as they did at that tender age—and I can truly say now without hesitation that this is true!

ABOUT THE AUTHOR

MARILYN L. THOMPSON IS CURRENTLY active as a free-lance pianist, organist, arranger, composer, and orchestrator. Her many sacred piano, organ, and vocal collections have and continue to be featured in major church publisher catalogues.